100 Ways to Get on the Wrong Side of Your Boss

(And Strategies to Prevent You from Getting There!)

Peter R. Garber

First Edition

Multi-Media Publications Inc.

Lakefield, Ontario

100 Ways to Get on the Wrong Side of Your Boss
by Peter R. Garber

Acquisitions Editor: Kevin Aguanno
Copy Editing: Josette Coppola
Typesetting: Tak Keung Sin
Cover Design: Cheung Hoi

Published by:
Multi-Media Publications Inc.
R.R. #4B, Lakefield, Ontario, Canada, K0L 2H0

http://www.mmpubs.com/

Copyright © 2006 by Multi-Media Publications Inc.

ISBN (Paperback):   1-895186-98-6
ISBN (Adobe PDF ebook):   1-895186-99-4
ISBN (Microsoft LIT ebook):   1-897326-05-X
ISBN (Palm PDB ebook):   1-897326-06-8
ISBN (Mobipocket PRC ebook):   1-897326-07-6

Published in Canada.

Table of Contents

Planning and Organization

Working Relationships

Assignments

Problem Solving

Feedback

Acknowledgements

I would like to acknowledge all of the bosses, both good and bad, that I have had over the past thirty years as each has helped contribute content to this book. Also, thanks to my wife Nancy and daughters Lauren and Erin for listening to me complain about these bosses for all these years.

I would also like to acknowledge Josette Coppola for another excellent copy editing job and Cheung Hoi for his wonderful cover design that captured the true essence of this book. I suspect that we have all worked for this boss at one time or another!

Preface

"I finally found a title that truly describes what I am qualified to write a book about!"

Peter R. Garber

Late one night on a flight returning home from a business trip, I was working on an early draft of this book. Engrossed in the project, I didn't notice that the gentleman sitting next to me was looking over my shoulder at my laptop computer as I wrote. It had been a long flight, and I suppose he had already read the airline magazine and in-flight gift catalog and had nothing better to look at.

"What are you writing?" he asked.

"A book about bosses and working relationships," I replied.

"What's the title?" he asked.

I told him I was still trying to find just the right title.

"Maybe you ought to call it *How to Be a Suck-Up*," he suggested.

I thought a lot about his suggestion in the weeks that followed. *Is that what this book is really all about?* I wondered. I finally came to the conclusion that there may indeed be some degree of "sucking up" involved in getting along with your boss. But is that really all that bad?

The conversation on the plane also got me thinking about a different way of treating the subject. While perhaps *How to Be a Suck-Up* was not exactly the title I was searching for, the stranger's suggestion made it clear to me that readers might enjoy and appreciate a more humorous approach to this topic. I realized that by -presenting the wrong ways to build a stronger working relationship with your boss, the right ways might be understood better by contrast.

There are, in fact, many ways *not* to be successful in maintaining a positive and productive relationship with your boss. *100 Ways to Get on the Wrong Side of Your Boss* was written to illustrate these mistakes to help you avoid making them in the future. Each of the 100 ways also explains how you can turn potential negatives in your working relationships into positives. So much of being successful is learning how to prevent failure. By gaining a better understanding of what can negatively affect your personal interactions at work, you can learn to build a stronger, more productive relationship with your boss.

100 Ways to Get on the Wrong Side of Your Boss was designed to help you develop a variety of approaches and plans for achieving this worthwhile goal of a better working relationship with your boss. Many of the strategies it presents can also be used to improve communications with your coworkers, as the underlying principles apply to people at all levels of an organization. For example, some of the suggestions involve extending the same courtesies to your boss that you would to anyone else. Just because someone is your boss does not mean you should treat him or her worse than you would other people. To the contrary, shouldn't you grant your boss equal or even greater consideration? Somehow, the concept of offering your boss these same common courtesies often gets lost in the supervisor-subordinate relationship for a variety of reasons.

The word "boss" conjures up many images for anybody that has ever worked for one. For many, the phrase "getting along with the boss" -may sound like an oxymoron. By their very nature, bosses are supposedly on the company's side, and their sole purpose may seem to be extracting as much work as humanly possible from those who report to them. For many employees, the title of Boss can be appropriately substituted for other names such as Tyrant, Ogre, Task Master, Attila the Hun or a variety of other more descriptive terms!

This, of course, is not the image you should have of your boss. Instead, you need to think of both of you as being on the same team. In many ways, you and your boss share the same goals and objectives. You need to look for ways in which you can support one another to make each of you more successful at work. By building a better working relationship with your boss, you strengthen both of your roles and positions in the organization.

Without this cooperative alliance with your boss, your success on the job can be seriously compromised, yet building such a relationship can be a difficult goal to accomplish. Getting along with people at work is not always easy, and sometimes you have to work very hard at it. There are so many ways in which your relationship with your boss can be affected. Today's work environment brings with it many potential conflicts due to the ever-increasing pressures to remain competitive. In the midst of all this stress, maintaining a positive working relationship with your boss can become one of your greatest challenges at work, and efforts to enhance this association may have to begin with you. If you depend on someone else to initiate this process, it may never happen.

100 Ways to Get on the Wrong Side of Your Boss is an invaluable tool for anyone who wants to begin this important process of strengthening relationships in the workplace. Each person's working relationship with the boss is different, just as each person wants different aspects of that relationship to change. This book provides you with a wide variety of ideas to enhance all your dealings with your boss. Even if you already get along well with your boss, this book can show you ways to improve this rapport. Customize these 100 ways as you choose to best fit your own situation. I hope that these ideas will inspire you to develop methods of your own to get along better with your boss and your coworkers.

Good luck, and may you and your boss work together better than ever to support one another and meet your shared goals for success in the future.

CHAPTER ONE

Communications

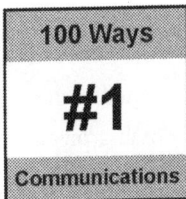

100 Ways	**Tell Your Boss Only What You Must**
#1	
Communications	

Tell Your Boss Only What You Must

Why should you give your boss more information than you have to? There are certain things you must disclose, but let your boss find out everything else without your help. After all, anyone that high up in the organization probably has better connections than you do anyway. Your boss should be the one providing you with information, not the other way around.

Problems Created:

- Your boss may be left in the dark

- Your boss may be misinformed

- Your boss will have to find other sources of information

- There may be less trust between the two of you

A Better Approach

True, there is a distinction between *need-to-know* information that your job requires you to tell your boss and *nice-to-know* information that you don't have to tell your boss. And it's up to you to decide how much to share. But many things that your boss does not *need* to know would still be *nice* to know, and it's this nice-to-know information that will be appreciated the most. Often, even seemingly insignificant information turns out to be critically important. Some things only become meaningful once other information is learned. Suddenly, the data may fit into a bigger puzzle or become the missing piece that you have been searching for. Just because something may not appear to be important to you does not mean that it won't be important to your boss. Let your boss decide what is important and what isn't.

100 Ways
#2
Communications

Leave Long Telephone Messages for Your Boss

Leave long, rambling telephone messages that force your boss to spend inordinate amounts of time finding out what you want. This way, maybe your boss won't have as much time to give you more work to do.

Problems Created:

- Your boss will waste time listening to your long messages

- Your boss may avoid your messages

- Your boss may skip important messages from you

- Your boss may think you are full of hot air!

A Better Approach

Unfortunately, this strategy probably won't work the way you intended. Particularly when sending recorded telephone messages to your boss, it is important to say what you need to say as concisely as possible. Most likely, your boss receives many messages each day and does not have the time or patience to listen to long messages that do not get to the point. Undoubtedly, your boss would prefer that you quickly make your point and hang up so that the next message can be accessed. Also, you need to realize that with most voice mailbox systems your boss has the ability to fast-forward or delete your message at any time. This is similar to operating your TV remote control at home—if you get bored with one channel, you simply click on to another.

Your boss might also check for phone messages at home. Wasting your boss's personal time will provoke even more irritation with you. Don't make your boss think of your messages as annoying commercials interrupting a favorite program. Rehearse your messages before you leave them. Practice until you can deliver your message in the least amount of time possible, and only then hit the "send" button.

100 Ways

#3

Communications

Tell Your Boss Last

Why is it that the boss is often the last to know? Perhaps everyone thinks that bosses are ˉso busy with other things that they won't want to be bothered with something else. Don't share information until you absolutely must, so your boss can concentrate on other matters more pressing at the moment.

Problems Created:

- By the time the news is heard, it may be too late for your boss to react

- Your boss may think that you are withholding information

- Your boss may have already made decisions without having all the necessary information

- Your boss will seek other more timely sources of information

A Better Approach

Tell your boss first rather than last. Don't make your boss the last one to know. When you have important information to share with everyone, give your boss the courtesy of hearing it from you first. Let your boss know that you are telling him or her first and what your plans are concerning communicating this information to others in the organization. This will let your boss know when it is appropriate to discuss this information with others.

Telling your boss first also builds a greater sense of trust between the two of you and saves your boss the embarrassment of not knowing something that everyone else at work knows. Your boss will feel better about the relationship with you and will appreciate that everyone else knows you entrusted him or her with this information first.

100 Ways
#4
Communications

Don't Tell Your Boss the Jokes Going Around Work

If you had to make your living as a stand-up comedian, you probably couldn't imagine an audience tougher than a roomful of bosses! Do you think your boss even has a sense of humor? Why even bother sharing the latest joke going around the office? Your boss probably won't think it is funny anyway.

Problems Created:

- Your boss probably does have a sense of humor and will lose out on enjoying a good joke

- You will miss an opportunity to share a laugh with your boss

- Someone else will probably tell the joke to your boss

- Your boss may think *you* don't have a sense of humor

A Better Approach

Yes, your boss probably does have a sense of humor and most likely would appreciate hearing a good joke once in a while—just make sure to keep it clean! It is important to your boss to be "plugged in" to what is going on in the workplace. Part of the culture of any organization is the humor that is created to help relieve the routine and stress that inevitably exists in any work environment. It is helpful to your boss's understanding of the mood or attitude of the people in the organization to share in the jokes going around, particularly when they relate to the workplace itself. Also, it is no fun when everyone else is enjoying a good joke and nobody will tell it to you. Who knows, your boss may tell you an even funnier story or joke!

100 Ways
#5
Communications

Be Insensitive to Your Boss' Problems

Undoubtedly, the last thing you have time to do at work is to listen to your boss's problems. You surely have enough of your own problems at work, most of which were probably created by your boss!

Problems Created:

- Your boss will think you don't care about other people's problems, including his or hers

- If you should have a problem, your boss may be less understanding

- Your boss may think you are insensitive

- You will miss an opportunity to build rapport and trust with your boss

A Better Approach

Even bosses sometimes need someone to talk to, so be a safe ear for your boss to bend. This means that you need to be a good listener. Be available when your boss wants to talk and encourage dialogue by being attentive and receptive. Allow your boss to express his or her feelings on certain issues, and don't be judgmental. Respect the openness and confidentiality of these conversations, and don't ever -abuse this trust that your boss has placed in you.

Let your boss know how much you appreciate sharing these feelings and that you are available to talk again in the future. As a result, you may have a better understanding of your boss and why things are done as they are at work.

100 Ways
#6
Communications

Don't Keep Confidential Information Confidential

Sometimes it's hard to keep a secret. People love to hear things before everyone else does, and it's especially tempting ⁻to tell other people what you have just heard. This is what is known in the government as *leaking* confidential information.

Problems Created:

- Your boss, as well as others, may no longer trust you with sensitive information

- The confidential information that is leaked may cause embarrassment or problems for others

- You may become known as the last person who should be told a secret

- Ethical or legal problems may result from your blabbing

A Better Approach

It could be argued that if two people know something, then it is no longer a secret. Confidentiality can be a very hard thing to keep. It is very important in your relationship with your boss for you to honor the confidentiality of information entrusted to you. The more your boss trusts your ability to keep private information private, the more information your boss will share with you.

Building this trust between you and your boss can enable you to receive critical information helpful in performing your job. But remember, this trust must be earned and can also be easily lost. Information is very powerful. When abused, this power -can be taken away and may not be easily regained. You could find yourself cut off from all kinds of communications. Consider what you may risk by sharing information that should remain confidential versus what you may gain -by honoring confidentiality. Help your boss learn to trust you with confidential information by keeping secret what needs to be secret.

100 Ways
#7
Communications

Let Your Boss Struggle to Remember Names

Have you ever known the name of someone at work that your boss was struggling to remember? Wasn't it fun to watch? Your boss was probably in torment, trying desperately to recall that name. If only you'd been asked for the person's name, you could have saved your boss a lot of embarrassment.

Problems Created:

- Your boss may embarrass others by not knowing their names

- Your boss will be greatly embarrassed

- Your boss may give credit or blame to the wrong person

- Your boss may forget *your* name someday

A Better Approach

Help your boss remember the names of other people in your workplace. Bosses often must deal with a wide variety of people as part of their jobs and sometimes need a little help remembering everyone's name. At any given time you need to be prepared to answer your boss's question, "Who's that?"

Particularly if you know that your boss is struggling to keep everyone's name straight, you might offer subtle reminders about each person. This can be done in such a manner that your boss may not even know that you are doing it. Mention people's names as they walk by or tell your boss specific details about people you work with. Before a meeting with people that your boss may not know as well as you do, review the names and backgrounds of everyone who will attend. Prepare lists of names of individuals that your boss will have contact with on visits to areas outside your workplace. Helping your boss remember the names of others will ultimately help him or her remember yours!

100 Ways
#8
Communications

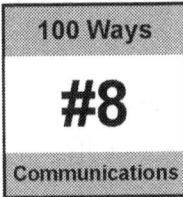

Don't Tell Your Boss How to Reach You on Vacation

Vacations and bosses seem to be contradictions in terms! The first rule about enjoying vacations is never to let anyone, particularly your boss, know how to reach you. When you're on vacation, your boss is the last person you want to even think about, much less get a call from.

Problems Created:

- Problems that you could have prevented may occur at work

- You may return to work to find a big mess

- Your boss might have to get involved in the details of your job

- Vacations may be a little harder to get approved by your boss next year

A Better Approach

The more your boss and coworkers learn to depend on you at work, the more difficult it is for them when you are gone. As much as you may hate to leave a telephone number where you can be reached while on vacation, your boss will greatly appreciate being able to contact you in case of an emergency. You may even call in to ensure that everything is going all right and that there are no problems that need your input.

Being accessible while on vacation will spare your boss and coworkers unnecessary trouble and may save you from coming back to a big mess. It is hard enough returning to work on the Monday morning after a vacation without having to face a mountain of problems caused by your absence.

100 Ways

#9

Communications

Never Let Your Boss Know Your Schedule

Moving targets are always harder to hit. Keep your boss guessing about what you are doing and when. This way your boss won't ever know when you are available to have more work piled on you!

Problems Created:

- Your boss won't know when you are working on something important and need to be left alone

- Your boss may not be aware that you already have too much to do and may give you more work

- Your boss may create more scheduling conflicts for you

- You may ultimately lose more control of your schedule

A Better Approach

You need to keep your boss informed concerning your schedule at work. Make sure your boss has the opportunity to know what you are doing and when. This may not always be necessary or important information to your boss, but there will be times when it will be appreciated. Your boss needs to know how busy you are to better understand what scheduling conflicts you might have with future assignments. Of course, this information may have little influence on how much more work your boss assigns to you!

If there are certain things that your schedule will absolutely prevent you from doing, your boss needs to be aware of this situation as well. Again, it is important that your boss be kept current on any scheduling conflicts so that solutions can be found. Your boss would much rather be told beforehand that you are unable to complete an assignment than be surprised by this news after it is too late.

100 Ways
#10
Communications

Ask Your Boss Questions that Can't be Answered

Let's play Stump the Boss. You know the rules: Ask your boss questions that are impossible to answer, just so you can enjoy witnessing the reaction. The object of the game is to see how uncomfortable you can make your boss with your questions.

Problems Created:

- You might embarrass your boss (even though that may be what you intended)

- Your boss might think you are prying into things that are not your concern

- You may be embarrassed by your boss's telling you to mind your own business in front of others

- Be careful what you ask for—you might hear something that you really don't want to know!

A Better Approach

Obviously, this is not the way to build a better relationship with your boss. There are many things that your boss knows but is unable to share with you. You probably have a pretty good idea what most of these things are, so don't put your boss on the spot by asking about them. If you do, don't be shocked by a response that sounds like, "I'm sorry, but that's confidential, and if I told you I would have to fire you."

You have to accept the fact that there are certain things concerning your workplace that you do not have a right to know, and for good reasons. By sharing these things with you, your boss would be betraying the confidence of those who divulged the information in the first place. Trying to gain this knowledge in ways other than through your boss is no different from espionage at work. The risks of getting caught by your boss are extremely high, and you can quickly destroy any trust your boss has in you by seeking information that is really none of your business.

100 Ways

#11

Communications

Be a Poor Listener

In our fast-paced communications age of today, it is virtually impossible to comprehend all of the messages we receive. There is just so much information being directed towards us via landline telephones, cellular telephones, voice mail systems, computers, ¯meetings, teleconferences and many other methods. How can you possibly listen to all of them, even if some of them are from your boss? Why even bother?

Problems Created:

- You may miss important messages from your boss

- Your boss will get the unsettling feeling of being avoided

- You will be "out of the loop" concerning communications from your boss

- Your boss may get used to being unable to communicate with you and stop trying

A Better Approach

In spite of all this competition for your undivided attention, it is important to be a good listener. Your boss needs you to digest a great deal of information quickly and accurately and may even expect you to be a better listener than those who work for someone else. Your boss may grant you less time and attention than others do, giving you important information quickly to save time in today's hectic business world.

Bosses appreciate employees who can receive and process information in this accelerated manner. The more you develop this skill, the more your boss will value your listening ability. When interacting with your boss, you may need to find ways to deal with these "turbo communications," such as taking notes or even developing your own shorthand methods. In this case, being a good listener may mean having a pencil and paper with you whenever you meet with your boss.

100 Ways
#12
Communications

Don't Give Your Boss a "Heads Up" About Problems

Is it really part of your job to tell your boss when there are problems looming on the horizon? Won't you be concerning yourself with things that really are none of your business by warning your boss about them? Just let these problems make their own ill-timed appearance. After all, do you really want to be the bearer of bad news to your boss all the time?

Problems Created:

- You will be neglecting an important responsibility if part of your job is to keep your boss informed about potential or actual problems

- Your boss will get information about problems from someone else

- You will have less opportunity to offer your boss solutions to these problems

- Someone else may get credit for keeping your boss informed

A Better Approach

If you know about an impending problem, -let your boss in on it. You may sometimes be in a position to hear about situations before they come to the attention of your boss. Of course, there may also be certain confidences that you cannot and should not share with your boss.

However, there are many other things that are appropriate and useful for your boss to know. Being forewarned about potential problems might help your boss minimize them or even prevent them from occurring. Consider any information that would not normally be available to your boss for some time and decide what would be useful to know ahead of time. Help your boss deal with problems in a timelier fashion by sharing this information as early as possible.

100 Ways

#13

Communications

Ignore Your Boss' Subtle Messages

How can you worry about your boss's subtle messages when you are already busy dealing with all those not-so-subtle messages in the form of assignments to get done? You may feel that you have all the messages you can handle from your boss without looking for more.

Problems Created:

- You may miss the most important messages from your boss

- Your boss will think you are very unobservant

- You might end up receiving very clear messages from your boss that you may not want to get

- Others in the workplace may be receiving the messages intended solely for you

A Better Approach

Often, bosses give us important information in very subtle ways, and if you don't pay careful attention you may miss them entirely. In this indirect manner, our bosses are telling us what they really want, as if they do not wish to shock or surprise us by simply coming right out and saying what is really on their minds.

If you want to understand what is important to your boss, listen for these subtle messages. By reading between the lines, you may find out what you really should be doing to meet your boss's expectations. The real message may be in your boss's body language or voice inflections. In other words, it may often be more important to concentrate on *how* your boss says something rather than on *what* your boss says. Try to pick up on what your boss really means, as these subtle messages may be the most important ones for you to understand.

100 Ways
#14
Communications

Hide Information from Your Boss

If you tell your boss everything you know, then you will not have any secrets anymore. Is this good or bad? Are there some things you really don't want your boss to know? Certainly there are, and you may decide that it is best to keep things this way.

Problems Created:

* Your boss may believe (rightfully so) that you are deliberately withholding information

* There may be less trust between you and your boss

* Your boss may become reluctant to share information with you

* The information may be more important for your boss to know than you realize

A Better Approach

You need to decide if you want to establish an open and honest working relationship with your boss or one based on deception and mistrust. How candid should you be with your boss? Well, how candid would you like your boss to be with you? Don't pretend that you are a guest on that old television quiz show, *I've Got a Secret,* and your role is to hide information from your boss. You should make a kind of pact with one another to share as much information that you can. If something comes up that you cannot talk about, simply tell your boss exactly that. Your boss will more likely understand and appreciate this need for confidentiality if you have an open and honest working relationship.

100 Ways
#15
Communications

Have Hidden Agendas

A hidden agenda is an underlying objective that is very different from what it appears to be on the surface. Sometimes people have secret motives that they disguise as something else. If you've ever been caught by surprise by a hidden agenda, you probably felt very deceived. As a result, you may constantly suspect that there is a hidden agenda lurking out there somewhere. Maybe you need to have your own hidden agendas to counterbalance the subversive tactics of everyone else at work, especially your boss.

Problems Created:

- Not everything will be "on the table" between you and your boss

- Your chances of implementing your agenda may be jeopardized if it is not out in the open

- Others, including your boss, may always wonder if you are being totally open and honest in your dealings with them

- Others, including your boss, may start hiding agendas from you

A Better Approach

Having hidden agendas will most likely only serve to create unnecessary suspicions in your dealings with your boss and everyone else you communicate with at work. Let your boss know what your true goals and objectives are in your work.

45

This way you can solicit your boss's support and the two of you can deal with each other in a completely open and honest manner.

Hidden agendas can be contagious. The best way to stop the spread of hidden agendas is to begin with your own honest agenda, an objective that is exactly what it appears to be.

100 Ways
#16
Communications

Don't Tell Your Boss about Changes

Bosses can sometimes become isolated from information about certain changes in their workplaces. These changes may involve events that have occurred in the lives of people at work, such as marriages, births, deaths, etc. Other work-related changes may be successes or problems that people are experiencing on their jobs or significant developments that are known by most people but would not normally "bubble up" to the highest levels of an organization. Maybe your boss is not supposed to know this kind of information, and you are going to keep it that way.

Problems Created:

- Your boss will be out of touch with what's going on in the workplace

- Your boss may fail to acknowledge changes in employees' lives due to ignorance about important events that have occurred

- Others may get the wrong impression about your boss's concern and caring for coworkers

- Your boss may get the wrong impression about *your* concern and caring for coworkers

A Better Approach

Is it your responsibility to keep your boss updated about these types of changes at work? Would your boss really be interested in hearing about these developments, and would knowledge of them be of any value? The answer is most likely "yes." These kinds of changes are important, and learning about them will make your boss more sensitive to what's happening in other people's lives, both on and off the job. Your boss will appreciate it if you pass on information about people and events in the workplace that is not typically shared with the boss. Maybe one day someone else will tell your boss about an important event in your life that may not otherwise have been known or acknowledged.

100 Ways
#17
Communications

Forget to Copy Your Boss on All of Your Important Correspondence

Do you really want your boss reading everything you send to other people? Do you have to tell your boss everything you do? The answer to both of these questions is most likely "no." Your boss would probably just question everything you said or how you said it. Save yourself this hassle by simply neglecting to copy your boss on your correspondence.

Problems Created:

- Your boss may be surprised at a later date by your correspondence

- Recipients of your correspondence might assume your boss knows what you wrote to them

- Your boss may think you are deliberately hiding information

- Your boss will be less likely to support anything that wasn't previously disclosed

A Better Approach

There are certain things you send to other people that your boss does need to know about. You want to avoid the embarrassment of someone else's assuming that your boss is aware of something you sent out when in fact you did not share the communication. Copy your boss on all your important correspondence, and let your boss decide what to read. The more important the recipients of your correspondence are, the more interested your boss will be to read what you have to say.

You may also want to consider soliciting input from your boss on certain important communications before you send them out. In this way, your boss will not only be aware of your correspondence but also be given the chance to support what you have to say.

100 Ways
#18
Communications

Avoid Getting to the Bottom Line

Try impressing your boss and everyone else at work with just how much information you can give them on a subject of great importance and urgency. Go into merciless detail on each point and avoid getting to the bottom line.

Problems Created:

- Your boss may stop listening to you after a few minutes if you don't get to the point

- The more you talk, the less impressed your boss may be

- You might hear snoring in the middle of your conversations with others, including those with your boss

- You may forget the point your were trying to make because of all your other chatter

A Better Approach

Bosses are typically very busy people and do not appreciate having others waste their time. Respect your boss's time by getting to the bottom line of the information you need to share as quickly as possible. You may be amazed at how fast this can be accomplished. It is helpful to forego many of the preliminaries that are normally part of accepted business etiquette, particularly when your boss is pressed for time.

By building a more comfortable and casual working relationship with your boss, you will find that you can exchange important information with each other in much less time. You do not always have to be as formal with your boss as you might be with others of your boss's stature that you know less well or deal with less often. However, you do need to be conscious of those situations when your boss may not want to rush to the bottom line. Let your boss make the decisions concerning how much an important subject or a particular point should be discussed. Your bottom line is this: Give as little or as much detail as your boss wants on any given topic.

100 Ways
#19
Communications

Send Your Boss an eMail about Him or Her by Mistake

Who hasn't sent an e-mail to someone by mistake at one time or another? Sure, you hope that the misdirected message doesn't contain highly sensitive or embarrassing information that the unintended recipient shouldn't see, but so what if it does? Imagine writing a scathing e-mail about your boss solely to entertain a coworker and then accidentally sending it to your boss instead. That could happen to anybody, and if it's a reflection of your true feelings about your boss, what's the big deal about an honest mistake?

Problems Created:

- You have created a written record of your negative feelings about your boss that is both indisputable and irrevocable

- You will have to explain why you were spending time writing caustic messages about your boss instead of doing your job

- Your boss will know how you really feel about him or her no matter what you say in your defense

- The person you meant to be the recipient may be dragged into this mess as well

A Better Approach

Never write anything in an e-mail that you would be ashamed or afraid to have your boss read. It's bad enough to bash your boss through office rumors that could be attributed to you, but putting your negative feelings into electronic words is even worse. An e-mail leaves an undeniable trail back to you.

If you are going to engage in critical commentary about your boss, choose a safer and more secure communication method. Remember, once you launch an e-mail message into cyberspace you lose control over its flight path. Most companies reserve the right to review employees' e-mails without the sender's knowledge to ensure compliance with company policies. Your negative remarks could be discovered as part of a company investigation having nothing to do with you, simply because you happened to send them to a particular individual. Once created, an e-mail may still be retrievable even if it is deleted.

So think carefully before sending out that nasty e-mail about your boss, regardless of how satisfying it may be at the moment. If for some reason your message finds its way to your boss, it won't seem so funny or clever if you have to explain why you sent it to him or her.

100 Ways

#20

Communications

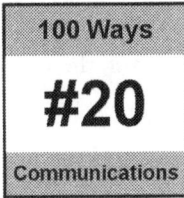

Surprise Your Boss

Some surprises in life are nice. Maybe you think that your boss's life could use a little more excitement. Who knows, springing a surprise every now and then about things that you're doing at work might break up the monotony of your boss's everyday work routine.

Problems Created:

- Your boss may not like to be surprised

- Surprising your boss may create a reaction that is not so pleasant

- You might be the one who is surprised when you get your next paycheck

- Surprise! You just really ticked off your boss!

A Better Approach

Most likely, surprising your boss would fall into the not-so-nice category, so remember, "It's not nice to surprise your boss!" Make sure that you inform your boss about anything that might potentially be a surprise. Think about what might be a surprise to your boss and make sure that he or she is kept informed about this kind of information.

It can sometimes be difficult to determine what your boss already knows about and what may be a surprise, especially when you are working closely on a new project or one outside your usual area. Thus it is easy to forget to promptly tell your boss those things that, when communicated too late, will only become a greater surprise. However, these surprises will not be pleasant ones for either you or your boss and should be avoided as much as possible.

100 Ways
#21
Communications

Be Evasive

By being evasive, you can keep from ever having to take a position on how you feel about any particular subject. This will protect you from controversy and conflict with others, especially your boss.

Problems Created:

- No one will know how you really feel about anything

- You may avoid conflict, but you will be a non-entity to others

- Eventually, no one will ask you for your opinion anymore—not even your boss

- Others may wrongly assume that you have no opinion because you lack the intelligence to form one!

A Better Approach

When it comes to dealing with your boss and coworkers, it's best to be frank and earnest. No, that does not mean that you should be two different people with your boss—Frank and Ernest—but that you should be honest and sincere about your views and opinions. Your boss needs to hear this perspective from you concerning what is occurring in the workplace. But you need to realize that there will be times when your boss may not like what you have to say, and only you can judge when this type of candor is appropriate and when it is not. Your boss sometimes needs to be ready to hear certain things before you share them.

As with so many other things in life, timing is very important when being frank and earnest with your boss.

100 Ways

#22

Communications

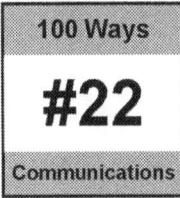

Expect Credit for Everything You Tell Your Boss

You should always expect to get full credit and acknowledgment from your boss when you provide information to be presented to other people. Why should your boss get credit for your knowledge and expertise?

Problems Created:

- You won't always get credit for what you tell others, so you will be continually disappointed if you always expect it

- The message might have more impact coming from your boss rather than from you

- Your boss will be reluctant to listen to you if you expect credit for everything you say

- Sometimes you may not want to get credit for certain things that happen!

A Better Approach

Making your boss look good without credit or recognition for your efforts is part of building a stronger working relationship between the two of you. You may find it helpful to offer your boss outlines of important points to make in reports or presentations relating to your job or area. No one knows more about your job than you do, not even your boss. By virtue of this input from you, your boss will make a better impression on those who receive or hear the information.

It is equally important that you allow your boss to take at least some of the credit for this knowledge. Do not expect any acknowledgment for being the source of this information (although it might be nice). Consider the transfer of this information to your boss as a gift that you should not expect to get back. This knowledge now belongs to your boss, not to you. However, you should feel a sense of satisfaction by providing this information, as you have made it clear how knowledgeable you are about your job and how valuable your input is to your boss.

100 Ways
#23
Communications

Don't Bother Telling Your Boss when You have Contact with His or Her Boss

You do not have to tell your boss when you have contact with his or her boss. After all, is it really anyone's business, other than your own? If your boss's boss wants to share this information, that's fine, but don't volunteer the news yourself. Your boss does not tell you about every encounter with this senior boss, so why should you?

Problems Created:

- Your boss may hear about it from the senior boss

- Your boss may wonder what you talked about with the senior boss that you're not sharing

- Your boss may be expected to know what you discussed with the senior boss

- You may have said something that your boss should know about

A Better Approach

Bosses like their own bosses to think they know what the people who work for them do on their jobs! Your boss will probably be very interested in what his or her boss had to say to you and will appreciate hearing this information. If you have contact with this senior boss, you will find that it is a good idea to communicate this to your boss. This will accomplish the following objectives:

1. It keeps your boss informed about what you are doing on your job and any new priorities that the senior boss may have created for you

2. Your boss will not be embarrassed by not knowing what the senior boss discussed with you

100 Ways

#24

Communications

Check for eMail and Voicemail from Your Boss Infrequently

In our electronic age of today, there are many ways to receive messages from your boss. Bosses expect you to keep current concerning the messages they send you, regardless of the method or format that is used. You could spend so much time checking for messages in all these various ways that your boss can send them that you won't have any time left to do your job.

Problems Created:

• You might fall behind in your work before you even get to the office

• You might miss important appointments or meetings because you didn't check your messages

• Your boss may have asked you to do something that needed to be done right away and you will be unaware of this

• You might be the last to know what your boss communicated recently via e-mail or voice mail messages

A Better Approach

Not checking your e-mail or voice mail messages frequently can put you way behind in your communications with your boss.

Although you may be thinking that this wouldn't be such a bad thing to happen, you could miss out on a great deal of important information. This could include meetings set up or canceled, arrangements changed, deadlines moved up or assignments sent to you. This last point deserves additional comment. You could be going about your normal routine without knowing that this huge assignment with your name on it has been floating around in cyberspace. Imagine your surprise if the next time you see your boss you are asked for a progress report on an assignment you don't even know exists. Maybe you should go check your e-mail and voice mail -for messages from your boss right now.

100 Ways
#25
Communications

Keep Your Boss Guessing

Remember being a kid and taunting your friends with that classic singsong refrain, "I know something you don't know"? The more you teased your playmates, the more they wanted to know the secret. Wouldn't it be fun to play that game with your boss? Just think how frustrated you could make your boss with this tune!

Problems Created:

*   This is not a game that your boss will enjoy

*   You might eventually be the big loser in this dangerous game

*   Your boss may decide to keep you guessing about things that are very important to you, like your job and salary

*   You could be the one eventually left out in the dark if you continue to hold back information from your boss

A Better Approach

It is never smart to play games with your boss, particularly guessing games. Don't amuse yourself by playing Twenty Questions and don't be coy or evasive about information that is important to your boss. Be direct and to the point about whatever your boss wants to know.

Avoid pretending that you do not understand what your boss wants to know when you really do. Relate as much as you know about whatever your boss is interested in hearing and, if appropriate, explain how you heard the information. Remember, you often reap what you sow, so if you don't want to be kept guessing about information that's important to you, don't play guessing games with your boss.

100 Ways
#26
Communications

Don't Tell Your Boss Your Career Goals

There are good reasons not to share your career goals with your boss. Your boss may tell you that you are crazy for even hoping to reach your target objectives. Or, if you aspire to a much higher position, your boss may feel threatened by you and may even sabotage your plans.

Problems Created:

- Your boss won't know your true career goals and aspirations

- Your boss may assume you want something in your career that is actually of no interest to you

- You may need your boss's support and assistance to reach your career goals, and you won't get that unless you share those goals

- Your boss may think you are perfectly content to stay in your current job forever and may not work towards your career advancement

A Better Approach

In reality, none of these perspectives will serve you well in reaching your career goals. Do not keep -these goals secret from your boss. Share your ambitions and seek support and input concerning your aspirations and how best to achieve them. With the help of your boss, develop both short-term and long-term objectives to map your progress towards your career goals.

Listen carefully to your boss's input concerning your plans. You need to realize that what your boss has to say about your career goals may not always be what you want to hear. You may receive honest feedback concerning how realistic your boss thinks your career goals are, and you have to make a choice regarding this input. You can accept this feedback and adjust your goals accordingly or you can decide that you can overcome any obstacles that stand between you and your goals. In any case, your boss can play an important role in your attainment of these goals. Ask your boss for training or assignments that will support your efforts to reach your career goals. Make your boss part of your career development process and work hard to achieve these objectives. Your boss's job responsibilities should include helping you progress in your career.

100 Ways
#27
Communications

Don't Tell Your Boss about Rumors Going Around

Everybody loves rumors and there always seem to be plenty of them going around the workplace. Bosses are not always included in the "rumor mill," probably because many people just don't feel comfortable spreading rumors to their bosses. Why? Maybe it's because the rumors are often about them! Why should you be the one to let your boss know what's buzzing around the workplace and run the risk of becoming a handy target for any anger about those rumors?

Problems Created:

- Your boss won't know what everyone's talking about

- Your boss won't know what might be concerning people at work

- Your boss won't be able to address the credibility of the rumors

- Your boss won't know if the organization needs to provide better communications to its employees

A Better Approach

It is important for bosses to understand what everyone in the workplace is talking about. Rumors usually contain some amount of factual information but can also be a gross misrepresentation of the truth. By sharing whatever rumors are circulating around the workplace, you give your boss the opportunity of addressing the accuracy of the information everyone is getting. Also, it is always nice to be "in the loop" about rumors, as it makes you feel more a part of what is really going on in the workplace and more in touch with everyone else. If not already plugged into the rumor network, your boss will certainly appreciate being included in it in the future.

100 Ways

#28

Communications

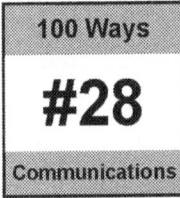

Don't Read What Your Boss Sends You

Many people rightfully feel that if they read everything that was sent to them at work, they would not get anything else done! So why bother reading what your boss and others send you? You have so many other important things to do. Every day you must make these kinds of priority decisions concerning what is the best use of your time and what is not. Besides, if your boss has already read the material, why should you? He or she can simply tell you what it is about.

Problems Created:

- Your boss probably expects you to be knowledgeable about what he or she sends you to read and will not be pleased with your disregard for this correspondence

- Your boss may test you on your familiarity or knowledge about what you've been sent

- You may be missing some very important information in the materials that your boss sends to you

- You may find yourself the only one who hasn't read what your boss sent out

A Better Approach

One of your priorities each day should be reading whatever you've been sent by your boss, who must have had a good reason for sending the information to you. Maybe your boss values your opinion and would like to discuss the topic with you at a later time or perhaps even wants you to become more aware of the subject and serve as the in-house expert in that area. Or it could be that your boss did not have time to read the material and wants you to summarize it. There could be many other reasons for your boss to send you something to read.

The bottom line is this: If your boss did not want you to read it, it would not have been sent to you in the first place. Read it!

100 Ways

#29

Communications

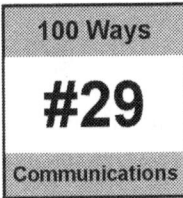

Be a Know-It-All

We all want to impress our bosses with how much we know about our jobs. Why should you hide your light under a bushel when you have so much to share? You're smart and you don't care who knows it!

Problems Created:

- You might not really know all the answers

- You will be disregarding the anatomy of successful business communication: You have two ears and one mouth, so use them proportionally!

- If you don't listen to others once in a while, you will never learn anything

- People will get tired of always being the listeners around you, even if you are right

A Better Approach

There is a difference between being knowledgeable and being a know-it-all. The biggest problem with know-it-alls is that they usually do not know it all. Don't try to tell your boss things that you are not really sure about. Stick to your own area of expertise and experience when giving advice to your boss. This is not to say that you should not offer your opinion on other subjects outside your area when asked or when appropriate to do so. The point is not to make a habit of speaking authoritatively to your boss about topics that you are unprepared to discuss. This is not the perception you want your boss to have of you.

Instead, focus your communications with your boss on what you do know the most about. If you want to expand your knowledge, then learn about other areas. But don't try to replace knowledge and experience with unqualified opinion.

CHAPTER TWO

Performance

100 Ways
#30
Performance

Don't Sweat the Details

Who has time for details anymore? Let someone else worry about them. Maybe your boss is interested in the details, but you have too many other things to think about.

Problems Created:

- You will make your boss worry about the details of your job

- Your boss won't have confidence that you are doing your job correctly

- Important details related to your job might be overlooked

- You may be shirking an important part of your job

A Better Strategy

There is an old saying in business, "You have to sweat the details to be successful." This statement implies that every aspect of the business is important and requires attention. Bosses have a tendency to worry about the details as well, and you need to sweat the details of your job. This is not something you want your boss to worry about. Your boss has plenty of other details of his or her own job to worry about and needs you to deal with your own details and be in control of them.

Don't fall into the habit or trap of depending on your boss to catch any details you have forgotten in your work. Make checklists for yourself of the important details of your work that must be completed. If your boss needs to have this kind of information, review your completed checklist with him or her. This way, your boss will be assured that you have taken care of the details and will have fewer things to worry about.

100 Ways
#31
Performance

Look at Work Only from Your Perspective

We all look at the world from our own perspectives. You view your job through your own eyes, so this is how you see your work situation and your place in it.

Why should you be concerned with how other people, including your boss, perceive the world in which you work?

Problems Created:

- You will only be looking at one side of the story concerning your job—yours

- You will have no idea how your boss may perceive your job

- You may be missing important perspectives of your job other than your own

- You will miss the opportunity to understand your boss and coworkers and how to get along better with them

A Better Approach

Remember the proverb, "You need to walk a mile in the other person's shoes to really understand where he has been." Imagine yourself in your boss's situation and position. How differently do you think things would look from where your boss sits? When viewing things from your boss's perspective, do you think that you would make some of the same decisions? How different do these same factors and circumstances look to you from your own position? How can better appreciating your boss's perspective help you understand and support your boss's decisions or actions in the future?

Talk to your boss about your different perspectives and how they affect the way you see the same things. Both of you will gain a better understanding about how each of you views the workplace and each other's positions.

100 Ways

#32

Performance

Hide Your Mistakes

Admit it: You sometimes make mistakes on your job. We all make mistakes, but no one wants them to be broadcast to others when we do. The last person we want to know about our mistakes at work is the boss. Perhaps we are afraid that we will appear incompetent or even stupid in front of our superiors. However irrational this thinking may be, it still prevails in virtually every work setting. What should you do? You could try to hide your mistakes, particularly from your boss, or you could try to blame your mistakes on someone else at your workplace.

Problems Created:

- You won't be doing anything to address any problems created by these mistakes

- You may be more likely to repeat these mistakes

- If your boss does discover the mistakes, the consequences may be worse for not reporting these problems yourself

- If mistakes are not corrected in a timely manner, they may become bigger problems

A Better Approach

We only make things worse if we don't acknowledge what we did wrong. Admitting our mistakes is the first step in preventing them from occurring again. When appropriate and necessary, review your mistakes with your boss and ask for support in helping you prevent them in the future. Whether it's ever acknowledged or not, your boss makes mistakes too and should be understanding of yours. Your boss will also respect your honesty and your commitment to preventing the same problems from recurring.

100 Ways
#33
Performance

Never Admit You Don't Know Something

Admitting that they do not know something can be difficult for many people, particularly when it relates to their jobs. We all want to be viewed as the resident experts in our job or field, so if we do not know something pertaining to our work we -may be defensive and reluctant to acknowledge this fact. We might -fear looking incompetent in the eyes of our bosses and coworkers. The solution to this dilemma is easy. If you do not know something, fake it. Pretend that you are in a poker game and bluff like crazy, so everyone else thinks you know what you are doing.

Problems Created:

- People will have less confidence in the accuracy of your answers

- You will eventually look more incompetent than competent to others

- You will only be able to fake it for so long before being discovered

- People will have less respect for you for never admitting you don't know than if you simply confessed your ignorance from time to time

A Better Strategy

The reality is that it is impossible for anyone to know everything about a job, and trying to bluff your way through life will only get you so far. As humans, we have limitations and deficiencies. No one, not even your boss, can realistically expect you to know everything concerning your job. Your boss will respect and appreciate your honesty in simply admitting when you do not know something about your work. However, you do need to follow up this admission with a commitment to obtain this knowledge, if necessary, and provide it as soon as possible. You will find that your boss and coworkers will accept this honest approach much better than an attempt to bluff your way through something you do not really know.

100 Ways
#34
Performance

Don't Worry About Quality

Quality is just another fad that management consultants came up with to sell their services to businesses. Like all other fads, it will fade away and -be replaced by yet another newfangled management philosophy. Why should you worry about quality when it is nothing more than a passing phase?

Problems Created:

- Your work will never promote your career goals until you realize that quality is not a passing fad and will always be important

- Your boss will not appreciate hearing about your sloppy work from others or seeing it firsthand

- There will be just too many negative consequences of ignoring quality at work

- You will be viewed as someone who has few or no quality standards on the job

A Better Approach

Quality is not something that can ever go out of style. Buzzwords relating to quality may come and go, but the principle of performing your job to the best of your ability and to the highest standards will always be in vogue. Pay attention to quality in all aspects of your job, continuously focusing on how you can improve the work that you produce.

Make your boss a part of your quality improvement plan by soliciting support for your efforts. Set increasingly higher standards for both yourself and your work product and monitor your progress. From time to time, review the data with your boss to make your commitment known and ensure that your standards are consistent with what's expected of you. Don't just give lip service to quality but instead make it an essential part of your job.

100 Ways
#35
Performance

Make Your Boss Your Copy Editor

Bosses are often very good at finding mistakes that are made by those who work for them. Why should you spend the time and energy finding your mistakes when you know your boss will correct them? Wouldn't this just be a duplication of efforts?

Problems Created:

- Your boss has better things to do than correcting your work and will not appreciate having to spend valuable time as your editor

- Your boss will think that you do sloppy work

- Your boss will think that you have poor written communication skills

- Your boss may wonder what other parts of your job need to be checked and reviewed

A Better Approach

Don't send letters and other documents to your boss until you have first proofread them and made all the necessary corrections. Your boss is not your spellchecker or copy editor. Even if you have a boss that is good at finding mistakes, do not fall into the trap of depending on someone else to catch your errors. Do you really want your boss to perceive your work as being full of mistakes and requiring editing before it is sent out?

Use your personal computer to check your spelling and grammar or ask a coworker to review your work before turning it in to your boss. When your boss is expecting to receive a final copy, -that is exactly what you should submit. Of course, you need to remember that your boss always has the right to make changes to your work. This is a boss's privilege. However, you still need to ensure that the changes your boss sees as necessary are not resulting from basic grammar or spelling mistakes that you should have found and corrected.

100 Ways
#36
Performance

Spend the Company's Money Carelessly

Everyone has heard, "You have to spend money to make money." What this advice means is that the more you spend of the company's money, the more the company will make! After all, it's not your money anyway.

Problems Created:

- Your boss will view you as wasteful

- Your boss may think you are equally careless about other aspects of your job

- Spending money won't always make more money, so your philosophy may be seriously flawed

- Wasting any resources, particularly money, will not be the best way for you to get ahead in the organization

A Better Approach

Money can seem to have a different value when it is not your own, especially when you are spending an organization's money. It might appear that a business has an endless supply of money to spend, particularly when comparing corporate funds to personal finances, but an organization also has seemingly endless financial obligations to meet. Your efforts to help your boss keep these expenses under control will be reflected positively. Keep good records of your efforts to save your company's money for future reference and as a possible reminder to your boss of your concern for your company's finances.

You can help support your boss in achieving these financial objectives by considering your company's money as if it were your own on the last day of the month before you get paid!

100 Ways
#37
Performance

Insist on Driving

When traveling on business, always insist on driving even if your boss would prefer to be behind the wheel. This way you can feel like you are in control and your boss will also begin to see you in more of a leadership role. This should do wonders for your career, right?

Problems Created:

- You may be evaluated by your boss on your driving skills

- If you get lost along the way, you may never live it down!

- If you happen to get a speeding ticket, you will really never live it down!

- You'll be the one that has to put the rental car on an expense report

A Better Approach

If your boss prefers to drive when the two of you travel together in a rental car, don't object. Being in the driver's seat is a natural role for your boss, and if you drive you will probably be subjecting yourself to more unnecessary critical evaluation. You will probably drive too slowly or too fast, take the least direct route, violate every traffic rule and park too far away from your final destination! Save yourself all this needless stress and hand the keys to your boss, saying something like, "You

know the way better than I do. Why don't you drive?"
Ultimately, everyone will be more satisfied with this
arrangement.

100 Ways

#38

Performance

Never Volunteer for Special Assignments

Why should you volunteer for extra work when your boss already has assigned you enough work to keep you busy for the rest of your career?

Problems Created:

- You may avoid extra work but you also avoid getting extra recognition and credit

- You may deny yourself a valuable developmental experience or opportunity in the future

- You may have enjoyed the different assignments and experiences

- Others may volunteer for extra assignments and move ahead faster than you in the organization as a result

A Better Approach

An old army motto advises, "Never volunteer for anything." While this may have been good advice at one time for those in the armed forces, it probably won't serve you well in today's workplace or in building a better relationship with your boss. Volunteering for special assignments can expand your horizons and perspectives. You never know where it could lead you.

Special assignments can expose you to parts of your organization you may never have seen. You can meet people you would not have contact with otherwise, which can help you build new working relationships. You can receive recognition for your extra efforts and create new opportunities for yourself that would not have existed without the volunteer work. Your boss will also recognize your willingness to do more than is normally required. However, a word of caution:

Make sure that your boss supports your involvement in these special assignments or your volunteer efforts may be viewed as a distraction from your normal responsibilities. You may want to give preference to those special assignment requests you receive from your boss over ones from others in your organization.

CHAPTER THREE

Planning and Organization

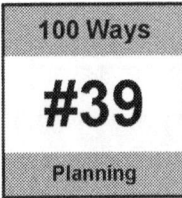

100 Ways
#39
Planning

Maintain a Poor Filing System

You may think that you do not have time to develop an elaborate filing system simply to keep track of things that your boss sends you. Perhaps your present system of putting these materials into a drawer or onto a pile on your desk works pretty well for you, and if it's not broken, why fix it? So is there really any need for you to change your filing system?

Problems Created:

- You will never be able to find anything quickly

- No one else will be able to find anything you have in your work area

- You may appear to be sloppy and disorganized to your boss as well as to others

- You will waste time searching for missing documents that would be readily accessible if filed properly

A Better Approach

If you spend more time trying to find things than doing anything else during a typical day, then maybe you should consider developing a better filing system. It is important for you to have a good filing system so you can quickly and easily retrieve the things your boss and others give to you. Bosses love to send things to those who work for them, and what they usually send is whatever they don't know what else to do with. The problem is that once in a while your boss will remember something sent to you and want it back. This can really put you on the spot. If you cannot find it—or worse yet, do not even remember what it is that your boss wants back—what does that say about how much attention you pay to what your boss sends you?

100 Ways
#40
Planning

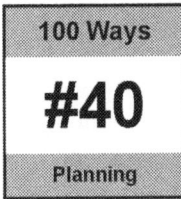

Don't Use a Planning Calendar

Who needs a planning calendar when all you have to do is remember a few upcoming dates and appointments? All you really have to know is where you have to be next and when. Why do you need some fancy planner or electronic calendar to tell you that? Once the appointment or event is over, why would you ever need to know anything about it again? Why would your boss or anyone else be interested in this information at a later date?

Problems Created:

- You may miss important meetings or events

- You will often find yourself in the wrong place at the wrong time

- Others won't be able to access your calendar electronically if you don't keep yours updated on the web or network

- You won't have any historical record of your past schedule for future reference

A Better Approach

There is any number of planning calendars or date books (including electronic or web-based ones) available on the market. If you are not already doing so, you will find keeping some kind of diary very helpful. These schedules can be an excellent reference concerning when certain events or important appointments took place in the past.

You may also find it helpful to jot down a few notes about these events as they occur that you think your boss might ask you about at a later time. Keep each planning diary for as many years as this information would be useful. Your boss and coworkers will soon learn to turn to you for the historical perspective on past business events and will appreciate your organization and resourcefulness.

100 Ways
#41
Planning

Be Late for Appointments with Your Boss

Being late for appointments with your boss will send the message that you are so busy that you do not have any time to spare, even for meetings with him or her. As a result, your boss will gain a better appreciation of just how valuable your time really is and try harder not to waste it by setting up meetings or appointments with you.

Problems Created:

- Your boss won't think you value his or her time

- Your boss will think that you can't keep yourself on a schedule

- Your boss may wonder what other commitments or obligations you fail to meet

- You will have less time to spend with your boss because of the time you have wasted by being late (this is not a good thing!)

A Better Approach

When you are late for an appointment with your boss you might as well say, "I don't value your time and think nothing of wasting it while you wait for me to arrive for our meeting. Furthermore, I am so disorganized that I can't keep track of where I am supposed to be and when. Also, I don't manage priorities very well." Is this the message you really want to be sending your boss?

Being on time and prepared for appointments with your boss will send just the opposite message. This will set the tone for the meeting and help both of you to be more productive during the time you spend together. Your boss will learn to appreciate your punctuality and consideration for his or her busy schedule.

100 Ways

#42

Planning

Never Keep a Copy of What you Send to Your Boss

Why should you keep a copy of what you send your boss? After all, you have already seen the document, so it is your boss who needs to have this information. Let your boss worry about filing this correspondence.

Problems Created:

- You may miss an opportunity to impress your boss with your thoroughness and organizational skills

- There may be no copy of what you sent your boss still in existence

- Your boss may blame you for both losing his or her copy and not keeping a copy of your own

- You won't have the benefit of the information contained in the document for whatever task you were trying to complete

A Better Approach

How do you know your boss will always have the information when you need it? Start a file to hold copies of everything that you send to your boss. Don't assume that your boss will save everything (or anything) you have sent. This way when you need to reference something you sent to your boss, you will be sure to have a copy. You will find this to be an invaluable procedure for you to follow. Your boss will be impressed with your resourcefulness and organization. You will also have the documents your boss wants whenever they are wanted. It won't take long before your boss learns to depend on your file copies of what you sent to him or her.

100 Ways
#43
Planning

Don't Let Your Boss Know about Your Scheduling Conflicts

Why should you tell your boss about scheduling problems before they occur? Informing your boss that you can't meet all your commitments will only make you look bad. Who knows, maybe some miracle will occur and resolve all your scheduling problems. Don't admit that you have a problem until you absolutely have no choice but to do so. Your boss will just think you have poor time management skills.

Problems Created:

- Your boss won't understand why you are having scheduling problems

- Your scheduling problems may be worsened by your boss's demands on your time

- Your boss may not try to help you resolve your scheduling conflicts

- Your boss may think you are just "blowing off" appointments because you feel like it

A Better Approach

On the other hand, letting your boss know in advance when you might have scheduling conflicts, particularly when work will be late or will not get done at all, may prevent the problem from escalating. Again, before you go to your boss with your scheduling problems, make sure you have tried to work through all of your options or alternatives. Your boss needs to be aware of any inability to meet commitments made to other people. You don't want your boss to be surprised by these problems or to hear about them from someone other than you.

You need to have your boss's support if you are unable to meet commitments due to scheduling conflicts. It is much more difficult to get this support when you ask for it after the fact. Your boss will feel better about things that are undone or canceled if there was an opportunity to give input into this decision. Your boss will also be interested in what you plan to do to prevent this scheduling problem from recurring in the future.

100 Ways

#44

Planning

Don't Remind Your Boss about Important Upcomming Dates

If you realize that your boss has forgotten about an important upcoming ‑event or date, just adopt an attitude of "If my boss isn't going to worry about it, neither will I."

Problems Created:

- Others may be upset if your boss doesn't show up for the important event

- Your boss may get in trouble for failing to remind a senior boss of the important date

- The organization's reputation may suffer if your boss neglects important client commitments

- You might get the blame for any of the above outcomes

A Better Approach

Most important events relating to work require a certain amount of planning and organization. The earlier this planning is begun, the less panic and stress there is as the actual date of the event nears. It will serve you well to keep a calendar listing the date by which necessary actions must be completed at critical times throughout the year. By planning ahead for each upcoming event, you may prevent many problems from occurring. You can ensure that the facilities, equipment, people, etc. are available when you need them. By giving ample advance notice of dates of the events you are planning, you can avoid scheduling conflicts with other events. The benefits gained by advance notice of upcoming important events will make life so much easier for your boss, who would no doubt ultimately have to answer for any scheduling problems.

3 - Planning & Organization

100 Ways
#45
Planning

Keep Your Work Area a Mess

Are you like Oscar Madison in the television show and film *The Odd Couple*? Do you leave your things lying around? Is being neat and orderly extremely low on your list of priorities at work? Do you believe that you have more important things to worry about than keeping your work area tidy? If you answered "yes" to any of these questions, forget what anyone else thinks and just bask in the charm of your casually cluttered workspace. If your boss happens to prefer a more orderly work area, that's not your problem.

Problems Created:

- Your work area may create a bad impression about you

- Your messy area may get the attention of someone even higher up than your boss who asks, "Who's responsible for this pigpen?"

- You won't be able to find anything in all that chaos

- You may have things living and growing in your mess that you aren't even aware of!

A Better Approach

There are many good reasons for keeping your work area clean and neat. At the top of most people's lists would be efficiency. A neat working area is most likely better organized, more accessible when searching for items and generally safer than a messy one. A tidy workspace -creates a more pleasant work environment, as you feel more in control of your job when your surroundings are organized. Neatness also makes a better impression on other people, particularly your boss, whereas extreme clutter or disorganization attracts only negative attention.

One of those people negatively impressed by sloppiness is invariably your boss—or worse yet, your boss's boss. This is the kind of attention you can definitely live without. Your boss has enough things to worry about without being concerned about your messy -work habits.

Ultimately, your workspace is a reflection on you. What image do you want to project about yourself through your work area?

<table>
<tr><td>100 Ways</td></tr>
<tr><td>#46</td></tr>
<tr><td>Planning</td></tr>
</table>

Be Unprepared for Meetings with Your Boss

Do you really need to prepare for meetings with your boss? After all, you see each other all the time. It's really no big deal. Surely your boss doesn't actually expect you to prepare for your meetings together the same as you would for a meeting with someone else.

Problems Created:

- The meeting will be less productive

- Your boss may think that you never prepare for anything else either

- Your boss still has a great deal of influence on your success in the organization and you will be missing the opportunity to make a favorable impression

- Your boss may begin to wonder if it's even worth the bother of scheduling a meeting with you

A Better Approach

Sometimes, depending on your relationship with your boss, you may have a tendency to become more casual and perhaps even less prepared for meetings with each other. You should be just as prepared for meetings with your boss as you would for meetings with anyone else in the organization.

Write a brief outline or agenda of what you need to review with your boss and have any necessary back-up data available. Don't be deceived into believing that your boss expects less in the way of preparation for your meetings together. In reality, your boss probably expects you to be even more prepared than others. Although meetings with your boss may be more informal than those you have with others in your organization because of your familiarity, they are certainly no less important. Meetings with your boss deserve your time to prepare for them.

100 Ways
#47
Planning

Keep Poor Records

If your boss does not keep good records, why should you? Let others ⁻spend their time on this tedious task. Good record keeping may be critically important in business, but it requires a certain amount of time and patience, and most bosses have very little of either! But that's not your problem. Let your boss spend the time keeping good records—you have more important things to do.

Problems Created:

- There won't be a good record of what has already occurred for future reference

- You may have no way to prove your case should a question come up about your role in past events

- You may be in violation of company policy or perhaps even laws regulating types of records that an organization must maintain

- If you are ever audited, you will be in big trouble

A Better Approach

Your boss will appreciate it if you keep good records and will learn to depend on you to provide the background and historical information needed to conduct today's business. Keeping good records will also help you perform your job in a more efficient and quality-oriented manner. Most people (including bosses) believe that they do not have the time to keep good records. In reality, this is probably more a function of discipline than of time or schedule. Many of us typically spend more time trying to find information that has been lost than would have been required -to file it in a more easily retrievable way.

In the end, it is much more efficient and less frustrating to develop a system for keeping good records at the time events occur than to go back and try to reconstruct what happened at a later date.

100 Ways
#48
Planning

Don't Make Appointments with Your Boss

Your boss's time is valuable, but so is yours. Why should you have to make an appointment to see your own boss? You also have a busy schedule. Maybe your boss should make appointments to see you!

Problems Created:

- You may never be able to get in to see your boss

- If you do get to see your boss, you may be allowed very little time for the meeting

- Your boss may constantly check the clock, more concerned about another appointment than about the meeting with you

- Your boss may continually tell you, "I'm sorry, but I can't talk to you right now. I'm going to be late for an important appointment."

A Better Approach

This is not the way it is supposed to work. Your boss has limited time and a calendar that is probably more crowded than yours. You need to respect your boss's busy schedule. When you need to have a significant amount of your boss's time, arrange it in advance and mention the subject you wish to discuss. You need to be flexible and accommodating -about your boss's availability, and this may mean working through lunch or having early-morning or after-hours meetings.

100 Ways
#49
Planning

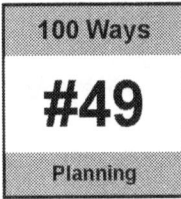

Get to Work Later than Your Boss

Why should you put more time into your job than your boss does? Who should set the standard for how early to report to work each morning, you or your boss? What do you have to gain by getting to work before your boss?

Problems Created:

- Your boss will always know when you are late

- Your boss will get a bad impression of you before you're even at work

- You will give your boss ample time to leave more work for you before you even get in the door

- If you also leave before your boss, he or she will know exactly how much time you put into your job each day

A Better Approach

Bosses seem to admire people they see already hard at work when they get there. As long as you beat the boss to work, it probably won't matter by how much or how little! Getting to work before your boss will give the impression that you are eager to get started each day. Spend this time in the morning getting organized and preparing for any business you have with your boss later that day. By the time you see your boss, you will be ready for your first assignment for the day. At the very least, you will have a few moments each morning to clear your head before you have to face the day and your boss!

100 Ways
#50
Planning

Schedule Your Vacation at the Same Time as Your Boss

Vacations are a time to relax and get away from all your troubles at work. Why should you worry if your vacation plans interfere with your boss's? That's ¬your boss's problem, not yours.

Problems Created:

- Vacation plans that interfere with your boss's plans may ultimately be your problem, particularly if your boss says that ¬both of you can't be gone at the same time. Guess whose vacation plans will most likely be cancelled?

- If you must reschedule your vacation, doing so may cost you time, money and the good will of anyone who planned to accompany you

- Your boss will think that you don't plan things very well

- If your boss's plans are canceled as a result of the scheduling conflict, there may be even more reasons to dread returning back to work the following Monday!

A Better Approach

There are at least two good reasons for planning your vacation around your boss's. First of all, you probably would not enjoy your vacation much if you knew your boss was mad at you because you both were away from work at the same time. This would surely make returning to work on the Monday morning after vacation even harder than it already is! And secondly, you get an extra vacation of sorts when your boss goes on vacation.

You may find that taking your vacation on the same week as your boss does is ultimately not the best use of your time. Find out as early as you can exactly when your boss is planning to go on vacation and arrange your own vacation around that schedule, not yours. Instead of being upset about any potential conflicts resulting from taking the same time off from work, your boss will appreciate your consideration. In the end, both of you will be happier if you put your boss's vacation needs before your own with the help of a little advance planning.

CHAPTER FOUR

Working Relationships

100 Ways
#51
Relationships

Don't Tell Your Boss about Your Conflicts with Others

Telling your boss about your conflicts with other people will just make you seem unable to get along with anyone else at work!

Problems Created:

- Your boss may only hear one side of the conflict, the other person's

- Your boss may prejudge who is at fault before hearing your side of the story

- Your boss won't have the opportunity to intervene in your behalf

- Your boss may get the impression that the conflict is bigger than it really is if the first account doesn't come from you

A Better Approach

Not telling your boss about these conflicts could make you look even worse. Make your boss aware of any conflicts you might be having with others at your workplace. Do not ask or expect your boss to take your side. Simply explain the situation to your boss as objectively as you can and let your boss know of any efforts you plan to resolve the situation. Ask for any advice your boss can offer to help you deal with the other individual.

Your boss will probably be much less concerned with the fact that you are involved in a conflict than with what you are doing to resolve the situation and prevent it from escalating into a bigger problem. Remember, bosses seem to have a knack for hearing about these things one way or another. It is better that your boss hear about any conflicts you might be having from you rather than from someone else.

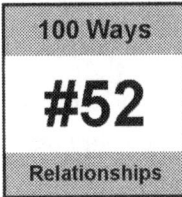

100 Ways
#52
Relationships

Be Moody

We all have our good days and our bad days. Try as you might, you can't always keep this fact from affecting your work. You can't be expected to go around all smiles and without a care in the world all the time at work. After all, you are at work!

Problems Created:

- No one will ever know how to deal with or approach you each day

- People may talk about your bad moods behind your back (doesn't that just tick you off and put you in an even worse mood?)

- People will whisper, "Be careful, (your name here) is in another bad mood today"!

- Your relationships with others may suffer because of things you say or do on your moody days

A Better Approach

Even if this is part of your personality, try hard not to be moody around your boss and other people at work. Leave your moods at home. When you bring your moods to work, you confuse your boss, who doesn't know if you are upset about something work-related (possibly something your boss did?) or something personal. All this gets in the way of developing a better working relationship between you and your boss.

Without knowing why you are acting a certain way, your boss cannot begin to address what may be bothering you at work. Instead of fostering a closer working relationship, you may end up pushing your boss farther away from you. Help your boss learn to understand you better by avoiding moodiness at work.

100 Ways
#53
Relationships

Don't Defend Your Boss

Why should you fight your boss's battles? Bosses can defend themselves without anyone's help. What do you have to gain by sticking up for your boss?

Problems Created:

- You will leave your boss "out on a limb" in the eyes of everyone else in the organization if you don't offer a defense

- People may expect you to defend your boss and view you negatively if you don't

- Your boss may hear about your lack of loyalty and be less than pleased with you

- You may miss an opportunity to express your support for your boss to others

A Better Approach

You have lots to gain by defending your boss and you should do so whenever possible. Don't let others misrepresent your boss's intentions or actions and challenge those who question them. When appropriate, let your boss know what the critics are saying and what you said in defense of the criticism. Talk with your boss to learn more about the background and basis of these criticisms and work together to correct any misconceptions that might exist at work regarding these harsh judgments. You can help your boss address the actions that are being justifiably criticized. The candid feedback that you provide your boss can be the first step towards correcting or improving these unfavorable reactions.

100 Ways
#54
Relationships

Don't Invite Your Boss to Join You for Lunch

You have to put up with your boss all day long, so why would you want to invite him or her to lunch when that's your one chance to escape for an hour of much-needed peace during the workday?

Problems Created:

- You will lose out on a chance to return late from lunch without any fallout

- You will miss an occasion to see your boss in a more relaxed state of mind in an informal setting

- You will skip an event that might offer the prospect of discussing things that you don't have time to address during the workday

- You may miss the opportunity to develop a closer relationship with your boss

A Better Approach

Maybe lunching with your boss is not such a bad idea. Typically, people wait for their bosses to invite them to lunch and don't consider extending the invitation first. You do not need to have a reason or an agenda to invite your boss to lunch, and in fact it is better if you do not have a motive. The fact that you initiated the invitation makes the occasion less businesslike and more relaxed. Lunch might serve as an excellent opportunity for each of you to catch up on what the other is presently working on, and it is worthwhile for the sake of improved communication alone.

If you're going to lunch with a group of people who also work for your boss, invite him or her to join the group. The invitation will make your boss feel more accepted by everyone and could make your workday just a little bit easier. Besides, your boss might even pick up the bill.

100 Ways
#55
Relationships

Treat Your Boss Differently that You would Treat a Friend

Bosses and friends represent two completely different types of relationships. Are there any similarities between how you treat your friends and how you deal with your boss? You treat your friends with kindness and understanding. Why should you treat your boss the same way?

Problems Created:

- Your working relationship with your boss may suffer

- Communications between the two of you might become almost non-existent

- Your ability to deal with stressful and difficult situations involving your boss may be impaired

- You may begin treating each other more like adversaries than collaborators

A Better Approach

This is not to say you have to be friends with your boss. What is important is that you extend to your boss the same type of courtesy that you would offer a friend. We help our friends in many ways: we listen to them, we care about them, we provide guidance to them, and we assist them with their problems and expect the same in return. Is there any reason why you cannot treat your boss in a similar way? What might be the benefits of establishing a relationship with your boss that is more like the ones you have with your friends? Remember, you often get what you give. Treat your boss (and coworkers) the same way you want them to treat you.

100 Ways
#56
Relationships

Never Give Your Boss the Benefit of the Doubt

A boss is a boss, right? Aren't all bosses the same? The only thing any of them are really interested in is getting more work out of you! Why even give your boss the benefit of the doubt? Would your boss do the same for you?

Problems Created:

- You will be constantly looking for negatives concerning your boss

- You may start treating your boss the way you would if the two of you weren't working for the same organization

- Sometimes you get what you expect from other people, so by expecting the worst from your boss you may get exactly that

- You might be grossly unfair and mistaken about your boss

A Better Approach

Cut your boss a break once in a while. Extend the benefit of the doubt rather than immediately assuming that your boss's intentions are not good. Remember, your boss also has a boss to answer to and may not always have much choice in the matter. Decisions may have already been made at a higher level and your boss may simply be carrying out another boss's orders.

Instead of giving your boss a tough time about ˉactions that must be taken, be supportive. Offer suggestions or volunteer for assignments relating to the work that needs to be completed. Encourage others to adopt the same attitude and avoid engaging in negative talk that does not support what needs to be done. Your boss may recognize your efforts in his or her behalf and appreciate your support in getting the necessary work accomplished.

100 Ways
#57
Relationships

Hold Grudges Against Your Boss

Grudges are resentments for wrongs done to us that we carry around like extra baggage. We hold on to these feelings of ill will as if they were "paybacks" for the problems that other people create for us. Grudges are often held against bosses and, at the very least, they can make us feel better because we believe we are getting even!

Problems Created:

- Your grudges may be apparent to your boss

- These grudges may reflect more negatively on you than on your boss

- Grudges will often beget counter-grudges

- The grudge may last longer than the validity of its original basis

Better Approach

Although grudges may have some useful purpose in life, they will not serve you well in your relationship with your boss. If you are carrying around grudges against your boss, you need to get rid of them before they weigh you down and create an obstacle to your future progress. Grudges ultimately hurt you more than the person they are intended to injure. Let the past be in the past and wipe the slate clean with your boss.

Freeing yourself of grudges is not something that anyone else really needs to know you have done. You might even mark the occasion with your own private "rite of passage." Although the reason may not be evident, your boss will probably notice a positive change in you once you have let go of your grudges.

100 Ways

#58

Relationships

Become Competitive with Your Coworkers

We all need to have some competition in our lives. A little rivalry makes us work harder to be better than our opponents. Your coworkers represent your competition in the race to get ahead at work. Winning in this contest depends on your ability to make yourself look better than others, especially in the eyes of your boss.

Problems Created:

- You may not be working as a team with your coworkers

- Your competitiveness may become counterproductive

- You may become less willing to cooperate with others

- It may become an "every man for himself" working environment

A Better Approach

Becoming overly competitive with peers who also report to your boss can put everyone in an uncomfortable situation. Your boss must consider the needs of all subordinates. Although some competitiveness can be good, too much rivalry can become destructive. Instead of watching coworkers waging constant battle, your boss would rather see everyone working together in a supportive manner to reach mutually beneficial goals.

Avoid becoming competitive with your coworkers and trying to convince your boss that you are better than the others. If you are better, your boss will know. Trying to prove the point only makes you look insecure and petty. Show your boss that you are a team player and you will ultimately stand out a lot more than you would if you tried to put yourself in the spotlight all the time.

100 Ways
#59
Relationships

Ask for Your Boss' Forgiveness Rather than Permission

There is an old saying that people in business have lived by for years: "It is easier to ask for forgiveness than for permission." As with many clichés, there is a great deal of truth in these words. By adopting this philosophy, you can do things that you could never have done ‐if you sought permission first.

Problems Created:

- This approach will only work a limited number of times

- You might end up with much stricter approval rules in your organization

- Your efforts may disregard reasons for not doing something that only your boss knows

- You will earn a well-deserved reputation for being deceitful

A Better Approach

While this strategy may work well occasionally, it is not a philosophy you should adopt very often when dealing with your boss. Granted, you may get away with it a few times, but your boss will quickly catch on to this scheme. If you continue in this manner, you can expect to hear very specific rules spelled out to you by your boss concerning the company's proper approval procedures to follow.

Instead of jeopardizing your integrity and credibility with your boss, make sure that whenever appropriate or necessary you obtain approval before proceeding with a course of action. Ultimately, the project will go much smoother and there won't be a "surprise ending" for your boss. Of course, there will still be circumstances when you have to ask your boss for forgiveness for something you did, but these occasions should be the exceptions and not the rule. You should explain your rationale for not keeping your boss informed -before and promise to try to prevent this type of situation from recurring in the future.

100 Ways
#60
Relationships

Run Things Past Your Boss Last

Letting your boss see things too early in the process may force you to change your plans before you really even get started. Maybe it would be better to keep what you're doing under wraps until you are too far along for your boss to change what is already done.

Problems Created:

- You may have to start all over again if your boss disapproves too late in the process

- You may waste time and money on something that won't be approved

- You may afterwards be told to inform your boss about everything you are doing in advance

- You won't get your boss's input when it can be more readily utilized

A Better Approach

It is actually a good idea to run certain things past your boss first. It is better to find out early how your boss feels about something than to wait until it is too late and much more difficult to change plans or direction. Ultimately, this will save you a great deal of time and the frustration of having to change what -has already been done.

You need to learn what is important for you to share and what your boss would prefer that you handle on your own. There is sometimes a fine line between what your boss wants to know beforehand and what you can initiate on your own. It may be best simply to ask your boss exactly what kind of information you are to disclose in advance and in how much detail.

100 Ways
#61
Relationships

Give Your Cold to Your Boss

Do you feel all achy and chilled to the bone? Are you stuffed up and barely able to breathe? Do you wish that it were someone else who felt this bad instead of you—maybe your boss? Drag your contagious self to -work when you're sick and make sure you sneeze a lot when meeting with your boss. This way your boss will end up feeling as lousy as you do. What a shame.

Problems Created:

- Your name may be used in vain every time your boss thinks about who passed on this cold

- Your boss may begin to associate you with feeling all achy and bad

- Innocent bystanders may needlessly suffer

- Misery loves company, but this won't be the company you really want to keep with your boss

A Better Approach

Here is some really good advice: Do everything possible to avoid giving your cold to your boss! Otherwise, you can be sure that for the next seven to ten days you will get the blame every time your boss coughs or sneezes.

If you have a cold, stay away from your boss as much as possible. Don't use your boss's phone and give ample warnings about the danger of using yours. This might be a good time to rely a little more than usual on e-mail or voice mail as a means of communication. If a few days after you come down with your cold you notice that your boss is coughing and sneezing or looking a bit peaked and pale, don't ask how he or she feels. You may hear more information about how your boss feels than you really want to know!

100 Ways
#62
Relationships

Complain More Often

Complaining is good for the soul, or at least that is what many of us think! If you don't ever complain about anything at work, maybe you should start. Of course, make sure that you take your complaints directly to your boss, who will certainly want to hear each and every one—so don't leave any out!

Problems Created:

- Your boss's biggest complaint may become you!

- Your boss may begin to think of you as a whiner and malcontent

- Your boss will take each subsequent complaint from you less and less seriously

- Your boss will begin to feel like the head of a complaint department

A Better Approach

Everyone complains about something from time to time. We all need to grumble occasionally to relieve some of the stress and frustration that come with our jobs, and complaining to your boss can be a productive way to communicate the problems you are experiencing at work. If you do not address these troubles, your boss won't be able to do anything about them. However, if you become a chronic complainer, your boss will become far less responsive to your problems.

Use complaints appropriately and sparingly. Do not run to your boss with everything you don't like or would like to see changed. Choose your battles carefully, making sure the issue is really important to you before you go to your boss with your gripe. Remember, your boss's capacity to be responsive to your complaints is limited. Don't turn into your boss's biggest complaint!

100 Ways
#63
Relationships

Don't Ask Your Boss for Advice

Asking your boss for advice may seem like admitting you can't handle your responsibilities yourself. It is tantamount to acknowledging defeat on your job. You might as well say to your boss, "I am incapable of performing my job without your help"!

Problems Created:

- You won't get the benefit of your boss's experience and knowledge

- Your boss may be less supportive of decisions you make if not involved in the process

- You will make yourself appear too proud to ask for advice

- You will set yourself up for hearing, "You should have asked me" from your boss

A Better Approach

If you view asking your boss for advice as a sign of weakness or failure, you are looking at your relationship with your boss in the wrong way. You shouldn't be afraid to ask your boss for advice, particularly in his or her area of expertise. You need to fully utilize all of the resources that are available to you, including your boss. There is nothing wrong with going to an expert for advice in a particular area, and if that expert just happens to be your boss, so much the better.

Your boss will feel good about being asked for input and is likely to be more supportive if included in your work process. You will be confident that you are moving in the direction in which your boss wants you to be headed. It is important that you get your boss's advice early enough in the project to be able to take full advantage of this expertise from the very beginning. This is much more desirable than being surprised by input from your boss during the final stages of a project. If a decision you make on your own turns out to be problematic, the last thing you want to hear your boss say is, "If you had only asked me, I could have told you not to do that"!

100 Ways
#64
Relationships

Ignore the Politics at Work

You can choose to ignore the existing politics at work. After all, you are not running for political office. Leave the politics to the politicians. Why should you concern yourself with such things that serve only as a distraction to you and take you away from your work?

Problems Created:

- You may be ignoring some of the most influential factors that exist at work

- You may be less able to get things done if you don't learn how to get the politics at work to work for you

- You will be less likely to understand why certain things are done the way they are at work

- You may be missing an opportunity to learn more about the politics in your organization

A Better Approach

Like it or not, some degree of politics is involved in every job. Politics in business means keeping your boss happy and keeping those who your boss works for happy and so on throughout the organization. In the politics of business, sometimes who you know is as important as what you know.

You need to have some understanding of the prevailing politics in relation to your boss's job. Politics may be an important factor in many of the decisions that have an impact on the organization and your career. Without considering the politics of an organization, you might expect decisions and events that are very different from what actually occurs. The influence of politics in an organization is a reality of business that cannot be ignored. You may not always understand or agree with the current politics, but there is probably nothing you can do to change the situation.

Ask your boss to explain more about the politics that must be considered in performing his or her job. Many of your boss's actions may make more sense to you with a better understanding of the politics in your workplace.

Correct Your Boss in Public

The more often people see you correcting your boss's mistakes, the more impressed everyone will be with you. Of course, your boss won't mind if you enhance your reputation at his or her expense.

Problems Created:

- You may be the one that ultimately gets corrected by your boss

- Others may not be impressed by your repeated efforts to make yourself look better at your boss's expense

- You may be wrong about what you think you are correcting

- Your boss *will* mind being constantly corrected by you and may take actions to stop this from occurring in the future!

A Better Approach

Maybe you need to think again before publicly correcting your boss.

You should never correct your boss in public unless it is absolutely necessary to prevent some worse event from occurring. Correcting your boss just to show you know something that he or she doesn't may make you feel good in the short term but will have negative consequences in the long run.

This doesn't mean that you should not ensure that your boss has current and accurate information or that you can't give your boss updates when information is outdated or wrong. However, the way in which you do this can have an important effect on your relationship with your boss. The less publicly you correct your boss, the more your input will be accepted and appreciated. Your approach has everything to do with how your boss accepts information from you. Find the best time and place to correct your boss and do it in a manner that is the most comfortable for both of you under these circumstances.

100 Ways

#66

Relationships

Try to Compete with Your Boss

Think of your boss as the competition and try to prove how talented you are by outperforming this rival to your success. As your defeated opponent, your boss will no doubt respect and praise your superior abilities. This is how it works on the athletic field and in battle, so why not adopt the same philosophy at work?

Problems Created:

- You may find yourself in a contest you don't want to win

- The only person you will ultimately defeat may be yourself

- If you think of your boss as the competition, you will already have lost

- You won't earn your boss's respect by trying to compete or defeat him or her

A Better Approach

Your boss is not the competition. If you try to compete with your boss, you will most likely lose. Impressing your boss is different from competing with your boss. You want your boss to support your efforts to be successful and not compete against them. Whether you have a competitive or supportive relationship with your boss depends mostly on you.

You have little or nothing to gain by trying to prove that you are as good as or better than your boss. You need your boss's support to do a better job and feel good about doing it, and your boss needs your efforts to ensure that his or her goals and objectives, as well as your own, are met. For both of you to succeed, you must each work towards a collaborative win/win scenario rather than an antagonistic win/lose situation. Make your boss your advocate, not your adversary.

100 Ways
#67
Relationships

Keep Making Your Boss Angry

We all have our own "hot buttons" that act like triggers to make us really mad. These buttons are usually pretty easy to find, especially if the person you're searching happens to be your boss. See just how angry you can make your boss. It may be a lot of fun for everyone to see your boss getting really stressed out and upset.

Problems Created:

- Your boss's anger may be directed at you

- You will constantly be putting your boss in a bad mood

- Your coworkers will also have to deal with the aftermath of your boss's anger

- An angry boss really won't be a fun person to be around

A Better Approach

Curiously, you will find people who are constantly pushing their bosses' hot buttons. They get into trouble time after time by doing this and then just keep coming back for more. Why do they do this? Maybe they just like to see their bosses get mad. Maybe they do not know any better. Maybe they do not want to ever get along better with their bosses!

Once you have identified what upsets your boss, you will know what to avoid in the future. Taking this idea a step further, you should not only steer clear of what makes your boss mad but also take steps to ensure that potential hot buttons are not pushed. For example, if your boss gets angry when you turn in an assignment late, make sure that your projects are completed well ahead of schedule. Most likely, timeliness will be appreciated as much as lateness is disliked.

100 Ways
#68
Relationships

Tell Other People's Secrets

Secrets are hard to keep. Who would it hurt if you told a few other people something that was told to you in confidence? After all, this is the type of "juicy" information everyone loves to hear.

Problems Created:

- Loose lips sink ships; ⁻others, including your boss, will stop trusting you with personal information

- You will become the "leak" in the organization

- People will be embarrassed to have private information about themselves spread around the organization

- You will be known as a "big mouth"

A Better Approach

Divulging personal information about people will hurt anyone even remotely connected to this information.   Let your boss know when you must honor the privacy of information that others have entrusted to you. If your boss knows that you have been asked not to share personal information about someone else, your reason for holding back this information will be clearly understood. This way, your boss won't feel that you are being evasive or deceptive in your dealings on the subject.

Your boss will also see that you take being trusted with personal information very seriously and will feel even more comfortable about sharing sensitive information with you in the future. If you can keep other people's confidences, it will be obvious that you can respect your boss's confidences as well. This is a very important factor in building a relationship with your boss that is based on trust.

100 Ways
#69
Relationships

Make Unrealistic Requests

We've all heard the adage, "If you don't ask for it, you'll never get it." We're all also acquainted with the negotiating strategy of asking for more than you ever expect to get. Familiarity with this approach dictates that you should always make unrealistic requests of your boss, so if you need $10,000 for a project you should ask for $20,000. Then when your boss slashes your request in half, you will have exactly what you needed in the first place. This tactic works equally well when asking for a raise.

Problems Created:

- You won't always get half of what you requested—the entire request might be refused

- Your boss won't take your future requests seriously

- Your next requests may be scrutinized closely to make sure they are legitimate

- The accuracy of your work may be questioned in other areas

A Better Approach

Do not play this game with your boss. It is more important that you establish credibility in your requests to your boss. Analyze exactly what is required to complete the project and ask for exactly that amount. Demonstrate to your boss that what you ask for is what you really need. Consider any contingency money that needs to be planned for and include it in the budgeting process. This way your boss doesn't have to keep guessing how much you really need and how much of your request is part of this negotiating ploy. Bluffing might be a good strategy to use in a poker game, but not with your boss at work!

100 Ways
#70
Relationships

Try Getting Even with Your Boss

Wouldn't it feel good to get even with your boss just once for all the things you are forced to do at work? If you had the power, what would be the first thing you would do to pay your boss back? Think about all the things you would make your boss do, particularly those tasks you really hated to have assigned to you. How could you act on some of these ways to even the score with your boss?

Problems Created:

- Ultimately, you may not get even but end up with a loss

- Paybacks won't always work the way you hope or expect and may backfire on you

- Any momentary satisfaction you gain may be offset by permanent damage to your reputation and job standing

- Acting out your fantasy about getting even with your boss may end up as your reality of being unemployed

A Better Approach

In a battle between you and your boss, put your money on your boss! You can never really win an argument with your boss. Your -boss may not always be right, but he or she is always your boss! Do not start something that may cause you to win the battle but lose the war. Sometimes people have their own ways of "winning" in their dealings with their bosses, which may involve getting even in some way to make up for the anger or frustration they feel towards their superiors. This can be dangerous, even destructive behavior.

Don't play the "get even" game with your boss. Instead, discuss how you feel about these important issues. Your boss may not agree with you or take any different action but will at least have an understanding about how you feel. Ultimately, this will serve you better than getting even with your boss in some manner in the future.

100 Ways

#71

Relationships

Don't Think Like Your Boss

Don't even try to think like your boss. It will probably just give you a headache! Instead, make no attempt to learn what your boss thinks about important issues at work. Don't begin to better understand your boss's viewpoints and subsequent actions. Go on being constantly surprised by what your boss does in various situations.

Problems Created:

- Your boss will become frustrated by your lack of understanding about him or her

- You will be less likely to truly understand what your boss wants or expects from you

- You may seem to be out of sync with your boss

- You will continually encounter unpleasant surprises from your boss

A Better Approach

Everyone has a unique way of thinking, including your boss! Our thoughts are determined by an infinite number of factors, many of which we may not always consciously recognize. However, with time you can begin to better understand why others think as they do about certain things.

As you get to know someone better, you learn how that person feels about many different subjects. You become more aware of how factors such as background or experience contribute to these attitudes. Give some thought to how your boss will think about the things that are important to you at work. This will help you better understand and possibly even predict how your boss may respond to these issues.

Imagine how helpful it would be to know what your boss is thinking. You may not be able to read your boss's mind, but you can learn to better understand -some of the decisions that are made at work.

100 Ways
#72
Relationships

Don't Try to Get to Know Each Other Better

Why should you try to get to know your boss better? Is it even possible that you could ever become friends? If not, why bother?

Problems Created:

- You may not gain any insight into how to get along better with your boss

- You may constantly do things that irritate your boss without even realizing it

- Your boss may miss the opportunity to get to know you and to learn how to work with you more effectively

- There may be many misconceptions about each other that will never be addressed

A Better Approach

Sometimes people become close friends with their bosses, but this is not often the case. The superior-subordinate aspect to the relationship may preclude friendship, as the boss's authority to give orders and evaluate a worker's performance violates many of the basic principles of friendship. Becoming friends with your boss may not be as important as the two of you getting to know each other better.

The more you learn about one another, the better you will understand each other. By building a stronger relationship, you can help bring out the strengths in one another and work more comfortably together. You will find that treating your boss with the same personal regard that you give to a friend will help both of you enjoy a better, more productive working relationship. Even if you and your boss never become friends, act as though you were friends. You will find that in your relationship with your boss, you get what you give.

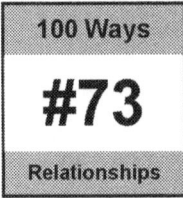

Don't Learn Your Boss' Habits

You don't have to pay attention to your boss's habits, so go on thinking that this is not important information for you to know. You don't have to try to understand what makes your boss happy or upset. You can ignore your boss's little idiosyncrasies and seemingly unimportant rituals.

Problems Created:

- You may be interfering with your boss's daily work habits or rituals

- It may be those so-called little things that really tick off your boss

- You may be constantly putting your boss in a bad mood by interfering with these daily work rituals

- Your coworkers may get upset with you for constantly upsetting your boss in this way

A Better Approach

Or you can decide to learn more about your boss and begin to better understand one another. Everyone has certain habits or patterns of behavior, and some of these habits are more predictable than others. If you are fortunate, your boss will behave in predictable ways, but if not, you have a much greater challenge. Learning to predict what your boss may do next in any given situation can be very helpful in working together more effectively.

With this understanding, you will be in a better position to anticipate and meet your boss's expectations and requirements. You can learn what your boss likes and dislikes in a wide variety of situations. Study your boss's habits and become an expert on predicting and dealing with them. These will prove to be valuable lessons for you to learn.

100 Ways
#74
Relationships

Be Controversial

Taking a controversial position on just about anything that you can think of will show everyone, including your boss, that you are an independent thinker. Don't worry about whether the controversy is needed or justified. Show your boss you won't simply accept the company line on anything.

Problems Created:

- Your boss may consider you more as a disagreeable person than as an independent thinker if you take this approach too far

- Your boss will avoid discussing potentially controversial subjects with you

- You may begin disagreeing just for the sake of disagreeing

- Always taking the opposite position or viewpoint probably won't help you get along better with others, including your boss

A Better Approach

Bosses generally do not like controversy. Their task is to run a smooth operation, and controversy can be counterproductive to this objective. Although some controversy is inevitable and may at times be helpful, your boss would probably prefer that you avoid continual controversy with others who work with you, and so would those people! Try to anticipate what causes controversy on your job and talk to your boss about how it might be prevented. This way, if controversy develops between you and others at work, your boss will understand your position better. Telling your boss when you are headed towards a potential controversy may keep you out of one with him or her. Learning when it is and isn't appropriate to be controversial can make all the difference to whether your boss views you as someone with strong convictions or simply a troublemaker.

100 Ways
#75
Relationships

Don't Tell Your Boss when You have Personal Problems

Never tell your boss anything about your personal life or problems. After all, your personal life is your business and what happens on your own time has nothing to do with work. Right?

Problems Created:

- Others, including your boss, may not understand why you are upset at work

- Your boss may attribute certain behaviors to incompetence rather than personal factors

- Your boss won't be able to provide you with support or assistance

- You may not have anyone to talk to concerning these problems

A Better Approach

It is important that you tell your boss and others when you are experiencing personal problems. This way, they will understand what other factors and outside influences may be affecting you on your job. The amount of details you share with others at work concerning your personal problems is entirely up to you. All they really need to know is simply that you are experiencing problems. Otherwise, they may misread any possible changes in your behavior or work as being caused entirely by factors in the workplace. You should also give your boss some kind of update or progress report on your problem and (hopefully) its resolution.

Your boss and coworkers will appreciate the trust you place in them by sharing this confidential information and will be more supportive of your personal needs during this difficult time in your life.

100 Ways
#76
Relationships

Hide Your Feelings from Everyone

Hide your feelings from everyone at work. Don't ever let anyone know what emotions you are experiencing at any given time. Keep everyone in the dark about what may be affecting you and your work. This way, your boss will believe that any problems you are having on your job are simply a reflection of your work environment rather than a consequence of being affected by outside influences!

Problems Created:

- No one will really understand how you feel at any given time

- Your opinions will not be known or understood by others

- How you feel about things is an important part of who you are, and this will be hidden from others

- You will miss the chance to help your coworkers, as sharing your opinions or feelings may help others better understand their own

A Better Approach

It is important to let your boss and coworkers know when you are frustrated, happy, angry, upset, skeptical, etc. concerning your job and work. Try to explain why you feel the way you do, so your boss and others will at least have some understanding about your emotional state. By better realizing how you might feel and react to certain situations or events, your boss can be more in touch with what is going on both in the workplace and with you. This is preferable to your boss's being forced to simply observe your emotions and behaviors without a clue as to what can be causing them. You will also feel better by getting things off your chest rather than letting them stay bottled up inside you. Telling your boss the way you feel about things that are bothering you may even be a first step towards resolving these issues.

100 Ways
#77
Relationships

Learn as Little as Possible about Your Boss' Job

Why should you concern yourself with anything about your boss's job? After all, you have enough to worry about with your own job. Learning more about your boss's job won't bring any benefit to you on your job, or will it?

Problems Created:

- You will be defeating your own interests if your boss's job is closely tied to your own job

- You may be hurting your chances of ever getting your boss's job

- You will never discover how understanding your boss's job may help you succeed at your own

- You will miss a chance to learn more about the reasons behind your boss's actions on the job

A Better Approach

It makes sense that the better you understand what your boss's responsibilities are, the better you will be able to support them through your work. Often, many of us actually know very little about our boss's duties and accountabilities. By learning more about your boss's job, you can gain a better understanding of what is most important to him or her concerning your own position. This is a very important dimension of your job, particularly to your boss. The more you can focus on these aspects of your job, the more you will be able to support your boss's own efforts in job performance.

100 Ways
#78
Relationships

Don't Worry about What Your Boss' Boss Wants

Why should you concern yourself with what your boss's boss wants? That's your boss's problem, not yours! Or is it?

Problems Created:

- Problems have a way of flowing downhill, so you will probably only be delaying the inevitable

- Problems that your boss's boss has now may become problems that you have later

- You will invite more trouble, as an upset boss is a problem for everyone in the organization regardless of relative level or position

- You miss the opportunity to increase your perceived worth, as helping to solve a more senior boss's problems will make you more valuable to your boss

A Better Approach

Nothing will make your boss happier than your help in getting along better with a more senior boss. Find out what is important to your boss's boss. What are some of the goals that your boss is expected to achieve and how can you find ways to support these objectives through your job? What information can you provide to help your boss communicate more effectively with this other boss?

Understanding more about what your boss's boss wants will help you appreciate the priorities and values of your boss's job. These objectives will undoubtedly cascade in some way to your job and work life. Helping your boss get along better with a senior boss can only help you get along better with both bosses.

CHAPTER FIVE

Assignments

100 Ways
#79
Assignments

Never Complete Assignments Before they are Due

As long as you get your work done on time, you won't have any problems, right? Why should you worry about completing assignments ahead of schedule? Will you get any extra credit or appreciation from your boss for the additional effort involved in finishing work early? Probably not, so don't bother getting things done before they are due.

Problems Created:

- Due dates have a way of changing and you may suddenly fall behind schedule

- Your assignments may begin to overlap, with newer ones behind schedule before they are even begun

- Your boss may needlessly worry that you are unable to meet deadlines if you never seem to be ahead of schedule

- Your boss may conclude that you are interested only in achieving minimum performance levels and not in assuming greater responsibility

A Better Approach

As you may have noticed, bosses tend to worry a lot about assignments being late. For many bosses, missing a deadline ranks right up there on their list of "sins" you should never commit at work. Late assignments can have a rippling effect on a number of other projects throughout the organization. This further multiplies the potential costs of your delays.

Save your boss and yourself all of this frustration and worry by completing your assignments before they are due. Usually, this is a result of your organizational and scheduling efforts rather than other factors that are out of your control. Make the practice of meeting due dates on your job a given and one less thing that your boss has to worry about. The sooner before an assignment is due that you hand in your work, the less your boss has to be concerned about it. Let your boss worry about getting someone else's work on time.

100 Ways

#80

Assignments

Don't Help Your Boss Do those Dreaded Tasks

Everyone has things they hate to do at work, even your boss. It is usually no secret what these tasks are, as people have a tendency to complain a lot about doing them! Listen to what your boss complains about doing and then decide: *Do I offer to help my boss get these dreaded chores done or do I just sit back and enjoy watching my boss miserably doing them?*

Problems Created:

- If you don't offer to help with these tasks, your boss might make doing them a regular assignment, so instead of a favor it becomes an obligation

- If forced to do these very unpleasant tasks, your boss may be very unpleasant to be around

- By trying to do these things alone, your boss may make matters worse and create a bigger problem for you

- Your boss will probably be more responsive to your needs if you offer to help with unpopular duties

A Better Approach

Think about ways that these things could be done more easily or delegated to someone else (hopefully not you if you feel the same way about the tasks as your boss). Try to be more supportive and understanding when you know that your boss has to do these detested tasks. Talk to your boss and find out why these duties are so objectionable.

If you do end up with these duties, do not complain about them to your boss or "lay a guilt trip" on your boss for delegating these responsibilities to you.

Instead, ask your boss for advice on how you can better perform these jobs. This will help your boss continue to feel involved in these chores and less guilty about passing them on to you. Remind yourself that you volunteered for these disagreeable tasks to build a better working relationship with your boss, and keep reminding yourself of this as you perform them.

100 Ways

#81

Assignments

Don't Do Your Homework

Homework sounds like something you left behind years ago when you were still in school. What does your boss expect you to do, pull an all-nighter to be prepared for the next project you are assigned? Homework is for kids and you already finished your assignments years ago.

Problems Created:

- You may be unprepared for assignments you are expected to be ready to do at work

- Your boss may start giving the more challenging and important assignments to others who do their homework

- You may not learn new things that can be important to your career advancement

- You might be making work even harder for yourself by not being prepared in advance

A Better Approach

Maybe you don't have to cram for midterms any longer, but you still need to be prepared for your assignments at work. It is important for you to do your homework at work. We never stop learning on our jobs and the lessons often do require a certain amount of preparation. If you don't have time during the workday, then you need to take your work home. Of course, there are circumstances under which you cannot possibly complete the work on the job and it is not practical to take it home. Your boss will understand these circumstances better if it is apparent that you are doing everything you can to get the job done, including taking work home whenever you can.

Doing your homework for your job can also involve simply being prepared for upcoming events. Most things require a certain amount of prep work. When this is not done, it is usually very apparent to everyone, particularly your boss. Many times this preparation does not involve a great deal of time but is simply a matter of doing it. If you ever do find yourself in a situation for which you are not prepared, you can always fall back on every kid's favorite excuse, "My dog ate it"! Don't laugh; it might be better than the excuses you are using now.

100 Ways

#82

Assignments

Don't Give Your Boss Updates on Projects

There are some very good reasons to avoid giving your boss updates on projects. First, by discussing assignments that are not completed you run the risk of having to listen to your boss's ideas about how you should handle the work. Secondly, you may have to answer questions about the project that you are not ready to answer. For example, if you are not sure how long it will take to finish the project or if you are behind schedule, you may be reluctant to give updates for fear that your boss will ask you about a completion date.

Problems Created:

- Your boss might be unpleasantly surprised when you finally give a status report on the project

- You may be wasting a lot of your work time doing things that your boss never intended for you to do

- You may find yourself with requested changes that you are unable to complete on time

- The longer you delay communicating the project's progress, the worse the predicament you might find yourself in with your boss

A Better Strategy

Regardless of these concerns, it is still a good idea to give your boss progress reports on the status of your projects. Your boss may also appreciate knowing some of the assignment details communicated in your updates. These updates may in fact become even more important if the project is behind schedule or if there are problems that your boss needs to know about.

Keeping your boss posted on developments helps you create and maintain a "no surprises" working relationship with each other. Your boss will be much more comfortable knowing the status of the assignments you are working on rather than having to wonder about it. Your boss will also be more supportive of your efforts to keep on schedule and more understanding about problems you encounter if these problems are discussed when they arise. Who knows, your boss might even have some good ideas that could be a big help to you with the project or could even help you finish it on time.

100 Ways
#83
Assignments

Wait to be Told to Do Things

As with volunteering, there may be nothing to gain by doing things before you are told to do them. Who knows, maybe your boss will decide that the work doesn't have to be done or will assign it to someone else. By jumping the gun you may just be creating more work for yourself rather than getting a head start on work.

Problems Created:

- Your boss will perceive you as someone who must be told to do a job rather than someone who can independently assume responsibility

- Your boss may assume that you have little interest in your job, which translates into little chance of being recommended for a promotion

- You will then be on your boss's timetable rather than your own

- You may have less time to get the work done than if you had volunteered earlier

A Better Approach

How do you think this attitude will serve you in your relationship with your boss? Probably not very well. Don't wait to be told to do things that you know your boss needs to have done. There is no sense in delaying the inevitable. If you are certain that particular tasks or assignments are coming your way, then just go ahead and get them done or at least begun. Holding off until your boss verbalizes an expected request will probably only put you behind schedule, as bosses are notorious for waiting until the last minute to give their employees assignments. By starting the work before your boss tells you to do so, you may be saving yourself from unnecessary problems that a delay would cause.

100 Ways
#84
Assignments

Miss Important Deadlines

Deadlines, deadlines, deadlines! It seems that our entire working lives are nothing more than a series of increasingly critical deadlines. Most likely, each of the assignments you receive from your boss has a deadline for completion that must be met. You could drive yourself crazy trying to meet every deadline your boss gives you. So why bother?

Problems Created:

- Missing a deadline may be very costly

- You may waste much time and effort, as some work has little or no value if completed late

- A delay in meeting deadlines may result in an inability to honor commitments, a particular problem if those commitments were made by your boss

- Missed deadlines are often very visible to others in the organization and may reflect poorly on both you and your boss

A Better Approach

You need to be concerned with deadlines, particularly those given to you by your boss. The consequences for missing these deadlines will vary depending on the project, but each one is important. If you foresee a problem in meeting an assignment deadline, let your boss know as early as possible. Be prepared to explain the reasons why you are behind schedule and the actions you have already taken, as well as your plan to minimize the delay. If you expect to receive similar assignments in the future, develop and share with your boss a strategy to prevent delays and then take the necessary corrective action. Do whatever you can to ensure that coworkers who are also involved in the project are committed to meeting the completion deadlines.

Deadlines are serious business to everyone, particularly to your boss, who will probably have to accept ultimate responsibility for your delays in meeting them.

100 Ways
#85
Assignments

Let Someone Else Make Coffee for Meetings

Let someone else make the coffee for morning meetings. Why should you be the one to brew a pot of coffee every time there's a conference? Don't you have more important things to do?

Problems Created:

- There may be no coffee for anyone to drink at the meeting

- As coffee levels drop, so do mood and productivity, so everyone's work may suffer

- If forced to make the coffee, your boss might make a big deal about it in front of everyone

- Your boss may make terrible coffee!

A Better Approach

What if everyone at work felt this way? How would coffee ever be made for meetings? Most people enjoy having a pot of fresh coffee ready when they get to a morning meeting. Regardless of your position, it would be nice if you let your boss know that you will make the coffee the next time there's an early conference. This is just one less detail about the meeting that your boss must worry about.

If you feel that it is demeaning to make the coffee, just get over it! It is a matter of taking care of a small but important detail that makes the meeting go as smoothly and productively as possible. Or would you rather have everyone be grumpy and nasty throughout the entire meeting because there was no morning cup of coffee?

100 Ways
#86
Assignments

Never Ask for Clarification on Assignments

How many times have you received an assignment from your boss and then later been totally confused about it? Maybe the assignment made sense as your boss explained it to you, but when you began working on it you realized that it was "clear as mud." What should you do? You have a number of options:

1. You could guess what your boss wants you to do

2. You could do what you feel like doing

3. You could do nothing

Problems Created:

- You won't know what your boss really wants you to do

- You will probably waste a lot of time doing the wrong things

- You won't meet your boss's expectations concerning the assignment

- The longer you wait to ask for clarification, the further behind schedule you will find yourself

A Better Approach

There is another option. You can ask your boss for clarification on the instructions. People are often reluctant to go back to their bosses and ask for clarification on assignments, even when they are unsure about what they are expected to do. Perhaps we are all afraid that we will look stupid in front of our bosses for not being able to grasp the instructions the first time. However, it is very possible—maybe even probable—that the instructions were poorly communicated and that clearly understanding them was virtually impossible. We are just making these poor communications worse by going ahead with the assignment without adequately understanding the instructions.

Regardless of how well instructions are communicated, take the time necessary to understand fully what your boss wants you to do. Review the assignment with your boss when it is given to you and do not leave until you have a clear understanding of what you are expected to do. In the end, both you and your boss will feel that this extra effort was well worth it and will be happier with the results.

100 Ways

#87

Assignments

Do Whatever You Want at Work

Wouldn't it be nice just to do the things at work that you feel like doing, completely ignoring what your boss wants you to do? Think about how much more effective you could be on your job.

Problems Created:

- You might be doing what *you* want but not what *your boss* wants

- You might not be working on what everyone else is focused on accomplishing

- You might work on the wrong things

- Most likely, you get paid to do what your boss wants you to do and not what you want to do, so you will not be doing your job properly

A Better Approach

Would you really be more effective on your job if you did whatever you wanted? How would you know if you were doing the right things to meet the requirements of the organization and your boss? How might this affect your career and future? Maybe having a better understanding of what your boss wants you to do is important. Do you really know what your boss expects of you? At first, this -question might sound a bit ridiculous. Of course you know what your boss wants you to do—it's what you do every day you go to work. Or is it?

Think about how much better you would understand what is expected of you if you sat down with your boss and developed mutually agreed upon goals for your job. This way, there should be no misunderstanding about what your boss wants you to do and what you actually do on your job. You will save yourself the time and frustration of going in a direction your boss didn't plan and will avoid misinterpreting the objectives of your job. Everyone, including your boss, will be more satisfied with what you do on your job.

CHAPTER SIX

Problem Solving

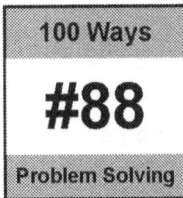

100 Ways
#88
Problem Solving

Don't Try to Work Out Problems Yourself

Why should you try to resolve problems at work yourself? Isn't that what your boss gets paid the big bucks to do? Besides, whatever answer you come up with will probably have to be changed to fit in with your boss's ideas anyway.

Problems Created:

- You may never learn how to solve problems at work on your own

- Your boss will think it's necessary to solve all your problems for you

- You may not always agree with or like your boss's solutions

- You won't know how to prevent these problems from recurring if you're not involved in resolving them

A Better Approach

Whenever someone takes a problem to the boss, probably the first question that is asked is, "What have you done on your own to resolve this situation?" The last thing your boss wants or needs is a desktop full of problems that have been dumped there by all the employees. Your boss probably has plenty of problems of his or her own without being burdened by yours.

Your boss will appreciate your efforts to work through your own problems on the job as much as you can. Ask yourself, "If my boss weren't available to approach with this problem, what would I do?" Consult your boss about only those problems for which the answer to this question is, "Without going to my boss with this situation, I will not be able to resolve it." Your boss will expect to be told about these problems and probably will not be upset with you if you cannot solve them on your own. Be prepared to explain everything you have already attempted to resolve the problem and to share your ideas on what your boss should do to remedy the situation.

100 Ways
#89
Problem Solving

Never Have a Contingency Plan

Why should you worry about things that will probably never happen? If you spend all your time planning for things that shouldn't happen, you won't have any time for what is supposed to occur.

Problems Created:

- You won't have a back-up plan

- You won't know what to do if things do go wrong

- You may be jeopardizing many resources by not having a contingency plan for unforeseen events

- Your boss will consider you ill-equipped to handle responsibility if you don't give any thought to unexpected developments

A Better Approach

Often it is wise to think like Murphy and assume, "Anything that can go wrong will go wrong." Always have a contingency plan just in case things do not go as you expect, and let your boss know about your forethought. Bosses worry a lot about things going wrong, so give your boss a little peace of mind by sharing your back-up plan. In the meantime, do everything you can to avoid the need to put your contingency plan into action. Both you and your boss will feel better in knowing that you have a fallback strategy. You will probably never have to use your back-up plan, but it never hurts to have one. Contingency plans make ¬your boss more confident in you.

100 Ways
#90
Problem Solving

Never Think Things Through Before Going to Your Boss

Who has the time to spend thinking things through before going to the boss in today's fast-paced business world? By the time you get done thinking about one problem, everyone else will have long since moved on to something else. By the time you find the answer, your boss may no longer be interested in the problem.

Problems Created:

- You will make your boss do your thinking for you

- You won't learn as much if you don't try to find your own solutions

- Your boss may think that you are not able to handle the more challenging aspects of your job

- You won't know what to do if you can't reach your boss

A Better Approach

No matter how busy you are, it is still important that you give matters thoughtful deliberation before discussing them with your boss. Make sure you have considered all aspects of the issue you plan to review with your boss. Think about what questions you might be asked or what additional information your boss may want and be prepared to respond. Again, don't make your boss do part of your job for you. That's what you get paid to do!

Of course, there are times when you should ask your boss to review something that you haven't been able to complete, and reasons for doing this include:

1. To keep your boss informed about what you are working on and any problems that need to be disclosed at the time

2. To obtain from your boss information that you don't have or directions about where to get it

3. To receive guidance, if this is something that your boss wants or expects to give to you

You want your boss to know that anything you bring to him or her has been thoroughly thought out and reviewed beforehand. Your boss's role is to offer any input that can help you, not to do your thinking for you.

100 Ways
#91
Problem Solving

Keep Repeating the Same Mistakes

Mistakes happen. Everyone makes mistakes at work sometimes because no one is perfect. If your boss understands this fact of life, there is no reason for you to be criticized for making mistakes, even if you keep making the same ones.

Problems Created:

- Everyone, including your boss, will get frustrated with you

- You will continually allow problems to occur that could be prevented

- It will make you look stupid in front of others, including your boss

- You may be subject to disciplinary action for carelessness

A Better Approach

Bosses get upset when they see the same mistakes being made over and over again but can usually find forgiveness within themselves when a mistake is made the first time. However, this understanding diminishes with each repetition of the mistake until it soon plummets to zero. When you make a mistake you need to follow these guidelines:

1. Get over it. Don't sit and brood over the fact that you made a mistake. And don't beat yourself up over it.

You are only human and we all are capable of making a mistake at work, even your boss.

2. Learn from your mistake. Consider it a great educational opportunity and analyze the contributing factors. What do you need to change about your work procedures? What should be changed in the system? What help and support might you need from your boss to eliminate similar mistakes in the future? What might you need to change about yourself to prevent future problems?

3. Don't repeat the mistake.

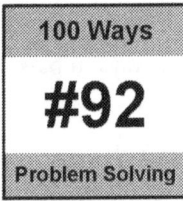

100 Ways

#92

Problem Solving

Pass the Buck

Round and round and round it goes, where the buck stops nobody knows. Is this the game that you play at work? Should you have a sign on your desk or in your work area that says, "The buck *doesn't* stop here"?

Problems Created:

- The buck needs to stop somewhere, and if it never stays where it belongs no one will ever have an incentive to correct mistakes

- Others might get blamed for your mistakes

- You will ultimately lose the respect of others if you are not accountable for your own actions

- You will be negligent in your duties, as accepting responsibility is an important part of your job

A Better Approach

But the buck has to stop somewhere. Take responsibility for your own actions. Don't try to "pass the buck" to someone else when it rightfully belongs to you. Your boss will respect your willingness to accept this accountability and is much less interested in who's responsible for a problem than in finding ways to resolve it. Your boss will focus attention on finding this solution and that is where you need to focus yours. Passing the buck only causes more confusion and wasted energy.

Of course, you will always find experts at buck-passing in any organization, and sometimes they will find ways to pass their problems on to you. Don't get caught up in their game and keep it going. Your boss is probably very aware of the buck-passing going on in the organization and is probably also aware of who takes care of things rather than dumping them onto someone else. Sometimes life is fair and buck passers get what's really coming to them while those who handle what they pass along get their just rewards.

100 Ways
#93
Problem Solving

Ignore the Obvious

For almost every task or problem at work, there are obvious things that could be done to correct the situation. But there usually isn't much glory in doing the obvious. You are looking for a way to really stand out in the crowd, to do something that no one else has ever tried. Besides, the obvious solutions have probably already been tried unsuccessfully.

Problems Created:

- You may be wrong in thinking that the obvious solutions have been tried already

- Sometimes the obvious solutions have to be tried repeatedly before they are successful, so you will miss the opportunity to utilize them

- The goal is to find solutions, not to impress your boss with how innovative you are, and you may be losing sight of this fact

- You may waste a lot of time trying things other than the obvious and best solutions

A Better Approach

It is important that you seek and exhaust all of the obvious actions and solutions to problems as they relate to your job. This is what plain old common sense should tell you to do! The problem is that often each person's common sense is different and what seems obvious to one person may not seem so to another. We can be blinded to the obvious and unable to see what is perfectly clear to everyone else. It is easy to ignore the obvious, particularly when we do not want to see it. Your common sense needs to guide you towards the same approach that conventional wisdom would dictate. You need to appreciate the perspective from which most others would see the issue or problem.

You should then decide whether you will pursue the obvious or embark on some other course or direction. However, it is highly likely that your boss will want to have a discussion with you concerning the obvious. Be prepared to talk about the obvious and your decisions concerning it.

CHAPTER SEVEN

Feedback

100 Ways
#94
Feedback

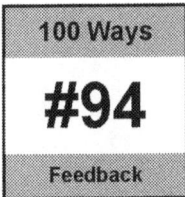

Never Give Your Boss Praise

Giving the boss praise? Isn't that getting things a little mixed up? Isn't it the bosses who are supposed to give praise to those who work for them?

Problems Created:

- Giving praise often goes both ways, so if you don't give it you may never get it

- By refusing to acknowledge praise-worthy work, you will miss a chance to impress your boss and your boss's boss with your positive work attitude

- Your boss may rightfully deserve the praise but will never get it

- Bosses need recognition from time to time too and will not be very pleasant to work with if they never receive it

A Better Approach

Be fair and give your boss any deserved praise. Let your boss know whenever you recognize those situations when commendation for certain accomplishments should be given and acknowledge these contributions to others you work with as well. Talk to your boss about his or her role and extent of involvement in the matter. Look for ways in which you might support your boss's similar efforts in the future and investigate other things that your boss should receive compliments for doing.

Don't be afraid to praise your boss for these accomplishments. Even bosses need to hear when they are doing a good job. Maybe a compliment coming from you will mean even more to your boss than one from a peer or supervisor.

100 Ways
#95
Feedback

Give Your Boss Nothing but Negative Feedback

Giving your boss nothing but negative feedback on how you feel about his or her job performance will certainly keep that ego from getting even bigger. This may also keep your boss from constantly trying to interfere with your work, leaving you free to do your job.

Problems Created:

- Your boss will get tired of your criticism

- Your boss may not always deserve this negative feedback

- It will look like you are just trying to make your boss look bad

- The negative feedback may ultimately be directed back at you

A Better Approach

This can be a tricky one. Your boss needs a balance of both positive and negative feedback concerning -job performance as it relates to supervising you and your work. Your boss needs to know exactly what helps and supports your work and what does not. There is no doubt that both of you can gain much by your boss's receiving this kind of feedback. The question is: How do you give feedback on this aspect of your boss's job performance? The answer is: Carefully.

The best way to give your boss negative feedback about job performance is to do it in such a way that it's not obvious that you are doing it! Letting your boss know about things that help you do your job better may be easy, but it's much more difficult to address those aspects of your boss's performance that don't support your work and job. Bosses have different tolerances for hearing this kind of feedback, and you need to judge for yourself just how much of it your boss will receive in a positive way. Your success in giving your boss feedback may be determined more by *how* rather than *what* you communicate concerning his or her job performance as it relates to you. Approach is everything when giving your boss negative feedback.

100 Ways
#96
Feedback

Criticize Your Boss Behind His or Her Back

Criticizing the boss is a favorite pastime in virtually every workplace in the world. We all love to talk about our bosses. We often vent our frustrations about our bosses by being critical about them with our coworkers. We all have our favorite tales about our bosses and sometimes play *Can You Top This?* with others when swapping stories. Go ahead and share your own stories about your boss with everyone at work.

Problems Created:

- Your criticism might get back to your boss

- You may be criticizing your boss unfairly

- Others may not agree with you and may resent your negative comments about your boss

- People might worry that you talk negatively about them behind their backs

A Better Approach

Have you ever thought what might happen if these stories ever got back to your boss and you were credited as the originator? This is the one time you do not want to be recognized as the inventor of something at work. What are the chances of these stories being traced back to you? They may be greater than you think.

Don't jeopardize such an important working relationship by criticizing your boss behind his or her back. It is not worth the risk. Find other more appropriate ways to express your frustrations about work. Remember, you never know when something you say may find its way back to your boss.

100 Ways
#97
Feedback

Don't Share Your Frustrations about Your Job with Your Boss

Do you believe that telling your boss how you really feel about your job would probably just be held against you? Is it better to keep these thoughts to yourself where they can't get you in any trouble? Maybe it is wiser to play it safe and keep your frustrations to yourself.

Problems Created:

- These frustrations will stay bottled up inside you

- Without knowing about your concerns, your boss won't be able to do anything about them

- Your boss may share these same frustrations and be wondering if they are a problem for you too

- Your boss might be able to suggest solutions that would alleviate many of your frustrations on the job

A Better Approach

It may be a better strategy to let your boss know both your negative and positive feelings about your job. Share your frustrations and discuss what you would like to see changed. Be fair and honest in your evaluation, as your boss needs to know what really bothers you about your job. Your boss may not be able to do anything to remedy the situation but at the very least should be more aware of your concerns and feelings. This way your boss will have a better understanding of your frustrations and their influence on your job performance.

Don't be reluctant to tell your boss what you like about your job as well. This might be just as important to share with your boss as what you don't like, as the information may lead to a better understanding of your motivations and ability to perform your job. The more your boss understands about how you feel about your job, the better he or she will understand how you perform your job.

100 Ways
#98
Feedback

Worry About Who Gets the Credit

Why should you let other people get the credit for your hard work? Make sure you get all the credit you have earned and deserve. Don't take the chance that your boss might try to credit someone else for your good ideas. Grab all the credit for yourself.

Problems Created:

- If you really don't deserve the credit, others will know, including your boss

- You may be denying credit to those who really deserve it

- Tooting your own horn won't impress anyone for very long

- Your coworkers will get tired of hearing you brag about yourself

A Better Approach

Don't be afraid to share your good ideas with your coworkers. Stop worrying about who gets credit for the suggestions and focus more on their implementation. Holding back your ideas will not benefit anyone, including yourself. Think about it realistically. What is the probability that someone is actually going to steal your good ideas and take all the credit? Most likely, other people will ultimately improve and enhance your ideas and deserve at least some of the credit for the final result.

Ask others to help you in implementing your ideas and give them positive feedback for their efforts. Nothing will ever change the fact that they were your ideas in the first place. Your boss will most likely know this as well and will remember where good ideas come from in the future.

100 Ways
#99
Feedback

Question Everything Your Boss Does or Says

Go ahead and question everything your boss says or does. This will make your boss scrutinize every decision and action in agonizing self-examination. By doing this, you will be helping your boss do a better job. Your boss will appreciate your constant questioning, right?

Problems Created:

- Your boss will quickly get tired of your constant questioning of everything

- You will often be needlessly wasting both your boss's time and yours

- Your boss will stop listening to your input

- Your boss may not always be right but is probably not always wrong, and your continual criticisms won't always be valid

A Better Approach

It is always easy to second-guess someone else's decisions. In hindsight, we might clearly see what should have been done if only we knew then what we know now. Consider the time and circumstances in which your boss has to make decisions. There may be reasons why certain things are done that ‑you have no idea about.

Don't fall into the negative mindset of questioning or criticizing everything your boss says or does. You could find yourself disagreeing just to disagree. This is not to say that you should never question your boss, but make sure that you are being accurate and honest about what you challenge. Be willing to agree with your boss when that is the way you really feel. You do not always have to have an idea that is better than or different from your boss's.

100 Ways
#100
Feedback

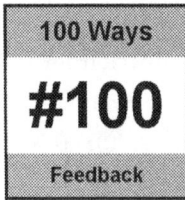

Ignore Your Boss' Feedback on Your Performance

Why should you pay attention to the feedback you receive from your boss concerning your job performance, particularly if it is negative? Your boss is probably just trying to keep you from expecting a decent raise this year! Then why should this year be different from any other?

Problems Created:

- You may be ignoring valuable feedback that would help you do a better job

- Your boss may conclude that you don't care about your job and may stop giving you any kind of feedback on anything

- What you will really be communicating is that you don't respect your boss's opinions

- You will just be giving your boss another negative to tell you about when addressing your overall performance for next year's evaluation!

A Better Approach

You need to keep an open mind when receiving job performance feedback from your boss. This may not always be an easy thing to do. Sometimes it is the most difficult feedback to receive that ultimately becomes the most beneficial. You have two options concerning how you accept feedback from your boss. The first is to deny that the information you receive is a fair and true reflection of your job performance. Or, as your second option, you can accept this feedback and possibly grow both personally and professionally. The choice is yours.

There are many factors that ultimately determine a person's acceptance of feedback from a boss. It is important to listen carefully to how your boss perceives your job performance, whether or not you agree with this appraisal. In this feedback is valuable information about what is most important to your boss concerning the way you do your job. Focusing on these factors can enable you to build a stronger relationship with your boss and improve your job performance and future evaluations.

About the Author

Peter R. Garber is the author of over 40 training, customer service, supervisory development, human resources, leadership and management articles and books. Mr. Garber has worked as a human resources professional for over 25 years in a variety of roles and positions. His expertise in career development has enabled him to develop the unique concepts and principles presented in *100 Ways to Get on the Wrong Side of Your Boss*. His recent books *Turbulent Change: Every Working Person's Survivial Guide, 10 Natural Forces for Business Success,* and *Winning the Rat Race at Work* also highlight Mr. Garber's creative approach to the many challenges facing employees and managers in today's increasingly challenging workplace.

Mr. Garber received his undergraduate degree from the University of Pittsburgh and completed his graduate work at St. Bonaventure University. Mr. Garber, his wife Nancy, and daughters Lauren and Erin reside in Pittsburgh.

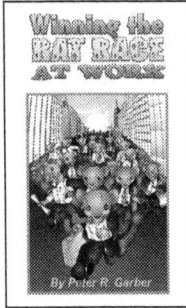

Need More Help with the Politics at Work?

Do you find yourself challenged by office politics, bad things happening to good careers, dealing with the "big cheeses" at work, the need for effective networking skills, and keeping good working relationships with coworkers and bosses? *Winning the Rat Race at Work* is a unique book that provides you with case studies, interactive exercises, self-assessments, strategies, evaluations, and models for overcoming these workplace challenges. The book illustrates the stages of a career and the career choices that determine your future, empowering you to make positive changes. A wealth of career management advice rounds out the book helping you with issues such as dealing with difficult bosses and coworkers by showing you how to identify and interact with different personalities at work.

Written by Peter R. Garber, the author of *100 Ways to Get on the Wrong Side of Your Boss*, this book is a must read for anyone interested in getting ahead in his or her career. You will want to keep a copy in your top desk drawer for ready reference whenever you find yourself in a challenging predicament at work.

Available in print and electronic formats. Order from your local bookseller, Amazon.com, or directly from the publisher at **www.mmpubs.com**.

101 Ways To Reward Team Members For $20 (or less!)

Kevin Aguanno

The Project Management Essentials Library

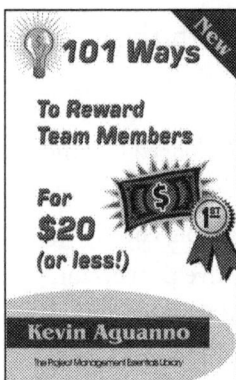

Your wallet is empty? And you still need to boost your team's performance?

Building team morale is difficult in these tough economic times. Author Kevin Aguanno helps you solve the team morale problem with ideas for team rewards that won't break the bank.

Learn over 100 ways you can reward your project team and individual team members for just a few dollars. Full of innovative (and cheap!) ideas. Even with the best reward ideas, rewards can fall flat if they are not suitable to the person, the organization, the situation, or the magnitude of the accomplishment. Learn the four key factors that will *maximize* the impact of your rewards, and *guarantee* delighted recipients.

101 Ways to Reward Team Members for $20 (or Less!) teaches you how to improve employee morale, improve employee motivation, improve departmental and cross-organizational teaming, maximize the benefits of your rewards and recognition programme, and avoid the common mistakes.

Available in print and electronic formats. Order from your local bookseller, Amazon.com, or directly from the publisher at **www.mmpubs.com**.

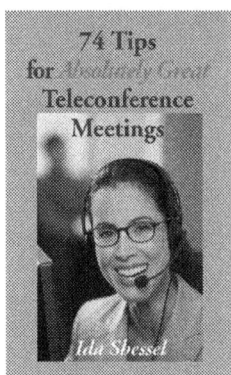

74 Tips
for *Absolutely Great*
Teleconference
Meetings

Ida Shessel

Become a meeting superstar!

With the proliferation of teleconference meetings in today's distributed team environment, many organizations now conduct most of their meetings over the telephone instead of face-to-face. There are challenges associated with trying to ensure that these meetings are productive, successful, and well-run. Learn how to get the most out of your teleconference meetings using these practical tips.

74 Tips for Absolutely Great Teleconference Meetings contains tips for both the teleconference leader and the participant — tips on how to prepare for the teleconference, start the teleconference meeting and set the tone, lead the teleconference, keep participants away from their e-mail during the call, use voice and language effectively, and draw the teleconference to a close. The book also includes a helpful checklist you can use to assess what you need to do to make your teleconference meetings more effective.

Mastering the art of holding a good meeting is one sure-fire way to get recognized as a leader by your peers and your management. Being able to hold an *absolutely great* teleconference meeting positions you as a leader who can also leverage modern technologies to improve efficiency. Develop this career-building skill by ordering this book today!

Available in electronic formats from most ebook online retailers or directly from the publisher at **www.mmpubs.com**.

Networking *for* Results

THE POWER *OF* PERSONAL CONTACT

In partnership with Michael J. Hughes, *The* Networking Guru, Multi-Media Publications Inc. has released a new series of books, ebooks, and audio books designed for business and sales professionals who want to get the most out of their networking events and help their career development.

Networking refers to the concept that each of us has a group or "network" of friends, associates and contacts as part of our on-going human activity that we can use to achieve certain objectives.

The *Networking for Results* series of products shows us how to think about networking strategically, and gives us step-by-step techniques for helping ourselves and those around us achieve our goals. By following these practices, we can greatly improve our personal networking effectiveness.

Visit **www.Networking-for-Results.com** for information on specific products in this series, to read free articles on networking skills, or to sign up for a free networking tips newsletter. Products are available from most book, ebook, and audiobook retailers, or directly from the publisher at **www.mmpubs.com**.

PM Audiobooks

The Project Management Audio Library

In a recent CEO survey, the leaders of today's largest corporations identified project management as the top skillset for tomorrow's leaders. In fact, many organizations place their top performers in project management roles to groom them for senior management positions. Project managers represent some of the busiest people around. They are the ones responsible for planning, executing, and controlling most major new business activities.

Expanding upon the successful *Project Management Essentials Library* series of print and electronic books, Multi-Media Publications has launched a new imprint called the *Project Management Audio Library*. Under this new imprint, MMP is publishing audiobooks and recorded seminars focused on professionals who manage individual projects, portfolios of projects, and strategic programmes. The series covers topics including agile project management, risk management, project closeout, interpersonal skills, and other related project management knowledge areas.

This is not going to be just the "same old stuff" on the critical path method, earned value, and resource levelling; rather, the series will have the latest tips and techniques from those who are at the cutting edge of project management research and real-world application.